You can never take what you love too seriously...

The Periodic Table Series

Periodically, we're all geeks about the things we love and the Periodic Table Series has been created to celebrate this universal fact.

Inspired by The Periodic Table of Chemical Elements*, our experts have applied scientific logic to an eclectic range of subjects that regularly baffle beginners and fire-up fans. The outcome of this experiment is the essential guide you hold in your hand.

Geeky? Absolutely.
Hugely satisfying? Categorically.

*The Periodic Table of Chemical Elements orders all the known matter that makes up our world, from hydrogen to helium, by chemical properties and behaviour to give scientists a handy overview of a rather complex subject.

Because it's always five o'clock somewhere!

THE
PERIODIC
TABLE OF
COCKTAILS

EMMA
STOKES

EBURY
PRESS

10 9 8 7 6 5 4 3 2 1

Ebury Press, an imprint of Ebury Publishing,
20 Vauxhall Bridge Road,
London, SW1V 2SA

Ebury Press is part of the Penguin Random House
group of companies whose addresses can be found
at global.penguinrandomhouse.com

Penguin
Random House
UK

Copyright © Ebury Press 2015
Illustrations © Hennie Haworth 2015

First published by Ebury Press in 2015

www.eburypublishing.co.uk

A CIP catalogue record for this book is available
from the British Library

ISBN: 978 1 785 03166 3

Printed and bound in China by Toppan Leefung

Penguin Random House is committed to a
sustainable future for our business, our readers
and our planet. This book is made from Forest
Stewardship Council® certified paper.

MIX
Paper from
responsible sources
FSC® C018179
www.fsc.org

Contents

The Periodic Table of
COCKTAILS

MARTINIS AND UP | DAISIES/ SOURS/CITRUS FRESH

←

	MARTINIS AND UP	DAISIES/SOURS/CITRUS FRESH		
APÉRITIFS	**1** Hp **3** Hanky Panky			
VERMOUTH	**2** Mz **5** Martinez			
VODKA	**3** V Vesper			
GIN	**4** Ma **2** Martini	**11** Av **4** Aviation	**18** Dd **6** Dill or No Dill	**25** Wl **4** White Lady
WHITE RUM	**5** Ep **4** El Presidente	**12** Da **3** Daiquiri	**19** Mc **7** Maid in Cuba	**26** Bs **4** Between the Sheets
TEQUILA	**6** Ls **3** Lost Steps	**13** Mr **3** Margarita	**20** Mt **3** Matador	**27** Ts **4** Tequila Sour
COGNAC	**7** H **4** Harvard	**14** By **6** Brandy Daisy	**21** Si **3** Sidecar	**28** Bc **6** Brandy Crusta
DARK/GOLD RUM	**8** Ro **3** Rum Old-Fashioned	**15** Tr **4** Treacle	**22** Jb **5** Jungle Bird	**29** Mi **6** Mai Tai
BOURBON	**9** Mn **3** Manhattan	**16** Br **4** Brooklyn	**23** Sf **4** Scofflaw	**30** Ws **5** Whisky Sour
WHISKY	**10** Rr **3** Rob Roy	**17** Bb **3** Bobby Burns	**24** Pe **4** Penicillin	**31** Ns **5** New York Sour
ABSINTHE	**81** Sz **5** Sazerac	**82** Rm **4** Remember the Maine	**83** Cr **5** Corpse Reviver #2	**84** Gf **5** Green Fairy
BEER	**91** Sj **5** St James's Gate	**92** L **4** Lagerita	**93** Db **6** De Beauvoir	**94** Sp **4** Shaky Pete's Ginger Brew
OVERPROOF	**101** Nm **2** Navy Martini	**102** Nd **4** Nuclear Daiquiri	**103** G **2** Gimlet	**104** Tn **4** Trinidad Sour

ELEMENT KEY
TOP LEFT: ELEMENT NUMBER
TOP RIGHT: NUMBER OF INGREDIENTS REQUIRED

#	Symbol	Superscript	Name
46	Bz	4	Britz Spritz
56	Az	3	Aperol Spritz
47	Ne	3	Negroni
57	A	3	Americano
48	Mm	3	Moscow Mule
58	Tw	3	Twinkle
66	Bm	7	Bloody Mary
73	Wr	3	White Russian
32	Bk	4	Breakfast Martini
39	Ss	8	Singapore Sling
49	B	4	Bramble
59	Tc	4	Tom Collins
67	Rs	7	Red Snapper
74	Ax	3	Alexander
33	Hd	4	Hemingway Daiquiri
40	Hu	6	Hurricane
50	Mo	5	Mojito
60	Cl	3	Cuba Libre
68	Cu	7	Cubanita
75	Pc	3	Piña Colada
34	Rc	4	Rude Cosmopolitan
41	Te	3	Tequila Sunrise
51	Ed	4	El Diablo
61	P	5	Paloma
69	Ba	11	Bandera
76	Df	5	Death Flip
35	Su	4	Sundowner
42	Fh	5	Fish House Punch
52	Fc	7	Fog Cutter
62	Am	5	Ambrosia
70	Po	7	Prairie Oyster
77	Eg	6	Eggnog
36	Pk	4	Painkiller
43	Pp	3	Planter's Punch
53	Sc	5	Scorpion
63	Ds	3	Dark and Stormy
78	Ru	3	Rum Flip
37	Kr	5	King of Roses
44	Bu	5	Bourbon Smash
54	Kj	3	Kentucky Mint Julep
64	Ll	4	Lynchburg Lemonade
71	Bd	8	Bloody Derby
79	Bo	4	Boston Flip
38	Bl	4	Blood and Sand
45	Al	3	Algonquin
55	Wc	3	Whisky Cobbler
65	Mg	6	Morning Glory Fizz
72	Bj	7	Bloody Joseph
80	Ic	4	Irish Coffee
85	Mk	4	Monkey Gland
86	Cw	7	Concealed Weapon
87	Af	3	Absinthe Frappé
88	De	4	Death in the Afternoon
89	Bf	7	Bloody Fairy
90	As	6	Absinthe Suissesse
95	Be	5	Best Bower
96	X	6	Drink with No Name
97	Ac	7	Ale of Two Cities
98	Bv	2	Black Velvet
99	M	5	Michelada
100	Gp	3	Guinness Punch
105	Z	10	Zombie
106	Nh	5	Nuclear Hurricane

Introduction

Welcome to *The Periodic Table of Cocktails*. The idea behind this book is to organise over 100 cocktails into a map of sorts, allowing you to explore the various types and categories of cocktails in terms of their similarities, but also their points of difference.

As well as including classic cocktails steeped in history alongside modern classics that feature on menus in bars the world over, I've included a few ultra-modern creations that you may not have heard of yet, but soon will.

Organising information into an easy-to-read format is a huge business. Look at any topic and it's likely you'll find a number of infographics that have been created to explain or explore the subject matter. The periodic table was perhaps one of the first examples of this, grouping and organising chemical elements so that their similarities were easier to see, and trends easier to deduce. As someone with a scientific background, the concept of using this structure to organise cocktails (my second love in life), was both a challenge and a joy.

Periodic tables of cocktails that have come before this book tend only to scratch the surface of what is possible, mostly just using the fact that a table is a cool way to display a number of cocktails, especially when designed as a poster for university bedroom walls! What I've done here is take the principles behind how the original structure of the periodic table organised the elements and apply them to cocktails to come up with something that not only looks good, but makes it easy for people to explore a multitude of mixed drinks.

Cocktail culture started in a time when global communications weren't that well established, so pockets of the world were innovating and growing alongside each other, often at the same time at different ends of the globe, particularly in London and New York. This means that there is often confusion about where some of the classics originated, what exactly is in them, and how they should be served. Some fantastic cocktails that appear in classic cocktail books such as Harry Craddock's *The Savoy Cocktail Book* (1930) or *Jerry Thomas' Bartenders Guide or How To Mix Drinks: The Bon Vivant's Companion* (1862) were not lucky enough to have been immortalised by a fictional British secret agent or womanising ad man. This book was therefore an opportunity to research the history of these drinks and to draw attention to those from past and present that I think equally deserve to be known. The remit: delicious cocktails with interesting stories and/or heritage.

The cocktail category is huge. There are so many spirits, liqueurs, juices and other ingredients that the possibilities are endless. With thousands of such possibilities, it can be daunting to know where to begin with a cocktail menu. What I hope is that, by using the table, people will be able to start with cocktails they know and love, and then move around the table to discover new drinks, with the flavours evolving as they go – yet still maintaining similar features to the previous drink.

How does the table work?

Each element in the table is a distinctive cocktail. They are then grouped into styles of cocktails in columns and by predominant base alcohol across the rows (the 'periods'). The cocktails get longer as you progress from left to right across the table, from the first column of martinis all the way to the collinses, fizz and snappers on the far right. In the rows, the spirits or liqueurs become 'heavier' as you move down the table. You'll therefore find vodka- and gin-based cocktails at the top, and bourbon and whisky-based cocktails towards the bottom.

The aim to all of this is that, if you like one cocktail in the table, you should like all the cocktails that surround it, as they will be of similar style and/or use a similar or the same base spirit. Next time you're glancing at a cocktail menu or working out what to concoct at home, you'll hopefully have the confidence to try something new and the knowledge to choose a little more wisely.

The three categories at the bottom of the table, termed the 'rare earth' elements on the original periodic table and separated from the main table, contain the more unusual types and styles of cocktails. They follow the same principles as the columns in the main table, so they get longer as you move from left to right, but rather than a predominant base spirit, they have other traits in common: the use of absinthe, beer or overproof spirits.

I hope you enjoy testing the table.

Cheers!

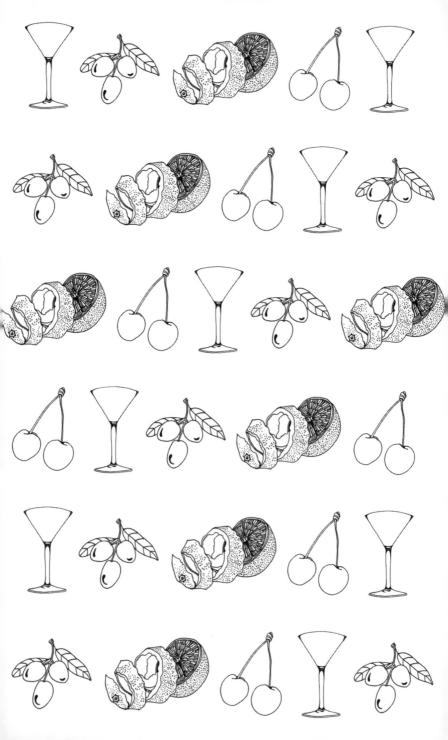

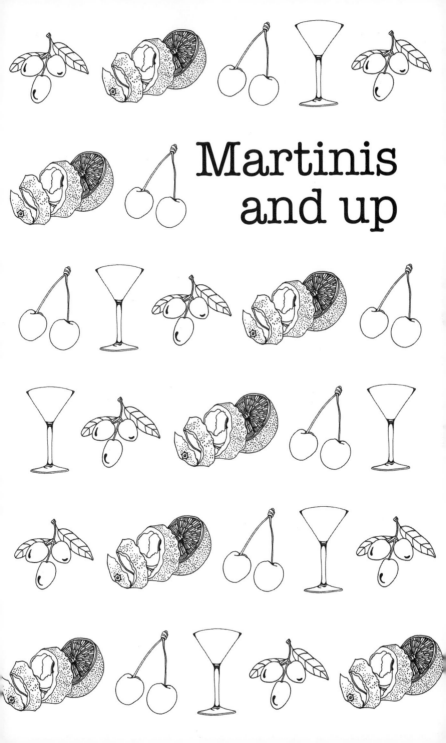

Martinis
and up

The cocktails in the first column of the table that are contained within this chapter can all be classified as martinis, or cocktails that are served straight up (i.e. with no ice). They're pretty serious in terms of their booze-heavy make-up, so you won't find any mixers or citrus here (with the exception of the Harvard, which has a dash of soda in it).

As they're mostly classic cocktails from bygone eras, drinking these drinks is akin to leafing through the pages of cocktail history, imbibing its past as you go and following a similar formula: of spirit, sweetener (vermouth, liqueur or syrup) and a bitter or herbal element, often in the form of cocktail bitters. The cocktails in this chapter are therefore almost exclusively stirred, the exception being the classic Martini, which can be made 'Bond-style' and shaken if you like, although traditionally would only have been made stirred.

The key to all of them is to use a good-quality base spirit, as this often makes up the majority of the drink. You also need to make sure that they're well chilled and properly diluted to make the alcohol 'sing' – and make them moreish-ly sippable.

They say a classic Martini should be consumed in three or four sips. I can see why: you don't want the drink to sit for too long and warm up to room temperature. However, as I mentioned, these are seriously boozy drinks, which most people (myself included) are likely to take more time over. There's a trick I've picked up from bars along the way, which is handy for drinks like this. Place a small vessel – a mini wine carafe looks the part, but may be difficult to get hold of, so a small bottle will also do – in a glass of crushed ice to keep it cool. Pour half of your cocktail into it, and the other half into the glass you're serving the drink in. This has the benefit of keeping half of the drink properly chilled without further diluting it, leaving you all the time in the world to savour your Martini, topping your glass up with the other half when you're done. Clever eh?

Column 1

1 **Hp** 3 Hanky Panky	
2 **Mz** 5 Martinez	
3 **V** 3 Vesper	
4 **Ma** 2 Martini	11 **Av** 4 Aviation
5 **Ep** 4 El Presidente	12 **Da** 3 Daiquiri
6 **Ls** 3 Lost Steps	13 **Mr** 3 Margarita
7 **H** 4 Harvard	14 **By** 6 Brandy Daisy
8 **Ro** 3 Rum Old-fashioned	15 **Tr** 4 Treacle
9 **Mn** 3 Manhattan	16 **Br** 4 Brooklyn
10 **Rr** 3 Rob Roy	17 **Bb** 3 Bobby Burns

HANKY PANKY

The Hanky Panky was created by Ada Coleman at The Savoy Hotel in London. Ada, or 'Coley' as she was affectionately known, was the first female head bartender of the American Bar in The Savoy in the early 1900s, at a time when women weren't allowed to drink in the bar. A bit of a rock star of her time, both for the cocktails she created, and leading the way as a female in a male-dominated industry, it is the Hanky Panky for which she is best known.

Consisting of gin, sweet vermouth and the Italian *amaro* Fernet Branca (a bitter aromatic spirit), the Hanky Panky is stirred down over ice, then strained and served straight up.

Created especially for Savoy patron Sir Charles Hawtry, an English actor, director, producer and manager, Coley recalled the story behind the cocktail to *The People* newspaper in 1925:

The late Charles Hawtrey... was one of the best judges of cocktails that I knew. Some years ago, when he was overworking, he used to come into the bar and say, 'Coley, I am tired. Give me something with a bit of punch in it.' It was for him that I spent hours experimenting until I had invented a new cocktail. The next time he came in, I told him I had a new drink for him. He sipped it, and, draining the glass, he said, 'By Jove! That is the real hanky-panky!' And Hanky Panky it has been called ever since.

Ingredients   30ml sweet vermouth
30ml gin
2 dashes Fernet Branca

Method   Put all the ingredients into a mixing glass with ice. Stir. Strain into a chilled Martini glass or Champagne coupe and garnish with a strip of orange zest.

2   5

Mz
Martinez

MARTINEZ

The Martinez is often touted as the precursor to the Martini. Whereas a Martini these days is made with dry vermouth and gin, the Martinez is a combination of sweet vermouth and gin (with added sweet liqueurs). When you consider that palates and tastes have moved from sweet to dry over the years, you can see why the Martinez is the perfect candidate to be the 'father' of the Martini.

Not only is there confusion as to its origins and its link to the classic Martini, so too is there confusion as to what exactly should go into a Martinez. Recipes for the cocktail appear in a multitude of classic cocktail books from as far back as 1884, in publications such as O.H. Byron's *The Modern Bartender's Guide* (currently thought to be the oldest recipe in print), *Jerry Thomas' Bartenders Guide or How To Mix Drinks: The Bon Vivant's Companion, Stuart's Fancy Drinks* by Thomas Stuart (1896), and Harry Craddock's *The Savoy Cocktail Book* (1930), among others. Each has a slightly different recipe for the Martinez; some even use dry vermouth rather than sweet. So, which should you make?

The recipe below is the way that I make a Martinez. I identify the cocktail as a sweet-vermouth-led cocktail that's designed to be a sweet cocktail overall.

Ingredients   40ml sweet vermouth
20ml gin
5ml maraschino liqueur
5ml orange curaçao
1 dash Angostura bitters

Method   Add all the ingredients to a mixing glass. Add ice and stir until well chilled. Strain into a chilled Martini glass or Champagne coupe and garnish with a small twist of orange zest.

3		3
V		
Vesper		

VESPER

The Vesper cocktail was immortalised in Ian Fleming's first Bond novel, *Casino Royale*. It is unique in terms of the cocktails featured in the Bond series, in that it was created for the book, rather than being an already established drink.

Some attribute the drink to Gilberto Preti, a bartender at Duke's Hotel in London, where Fleming often stayed. However, the dates don't seem to add up: cocktail historian Ted Haigh has researched extensively and has found no record of Preti working behind the bar in London until at least 1960 – well after the book was published. Despite the hazy history of its conception (an unsurprisingly common occurrence in cocktail history), Fleming enjoyed the Vesper so much that he included it in his first James Bond novel, going so far as to specify the exact ingredients, method and garnish.

A mix of vodka, gin and the now-discontinued apéritif wine Kina Lillet, the Vesper is shaken, not stirred, as is typical of the fictional British agent when it comes to his martinis. Since 1953, both Kina Lillet and Gordon's have been reformulated: the gin now has a lower ABV (alcohol by volume) and the closest Lillet equivalent is less bitter due to a reduced quinine content; therefore perhaps it makes sense to modify the ingredients slightly. You can use Lillet Blanc as the nearest substitute for the Kina, and any classic London dry gin with a decent ABV (i.e. over 40%) will work in a modern version of the Vesper. It is best served as cold as you can possibly get it, with the lemon twist over the top providing the drink with lift from the citrus oils.

Ingredients   60ml gin
20ml vodka
10ml Lillet Blanc

Method   Shake all the ingredients with ice in a shaker, and double-strain into a chilled Martini glass, or, as specified in the book, a goblet or wine glass. Add a lemon twist over the top.

MARTINI

The classic Martini is one of the most iconic and most-written-about cocktails in history. A simple double act of spirit and vermouth, this is a drink where the quality of the spirits you use is important, as they really get the opportunity to shine.

Gin or vodka?

The classic Martini is made with gin, which is why Mr Bond always specifies a 'vodka Martini' in his order. Any quality distilled gin with a decent ABV (i.e. above 40% alcohol by volume) will make a great Martini, and with the multitude of gins on the market at the moment, there are endless flavour possibilities, from the more classically styled London dry gins to newer formulations that utilise botanicals such as cucumbers, olives, herbs such as rosemary and thyme, and flowers such as rose, lavender and honeysuckle. The Martini provides the perfect opportunity for you to play around with your choices of brands and styles, so make the most of it and experiment!

Vermouth

Once you've chosen your gin, it's on to the vermouth. There are many different brands of vermouth, and it's the dry variation you're looking for to make a classic Martini. Some are drier than others; some bring a more floral or fruity flavour to the final cocktail. Trial and error is the best way to decide what to use. If you're looking for somewhere to start, though, you can't go wrong with the extra-dry version from Martini or Noilly Prat.

Wet or dry?

The next decision is whether you want your Martini 'dry' or 'wet'. This relates to the proportion of spirit to vermouth. Trends over the years have seen the Martini become drier and drier (less and less vermouth); however, a wet Martini can be the perfect introductory Martini, as it reduces the strength of the cocktail (although not the overall alcohol content). The recipe on page 13 is for a 6:1 Martini, which is a good place to start. Don't be afraid to play around with the proportions until you find your perfect ratio, though.

Shaken or stirred?

Never has a literary reference caused so much confusion than James Bond's order of his vodka Martini 'shaken, not stirred'. There are a number of points to clarify on this issue.

1) Any Martini can be made shaken OR stirred. Ignore anyone who tells you that shaking a gin Martini 'bruises' the spirit; it's a long-standing misconception. Ask yourself how you 'bruise' a liquid. A shaken Martini is definitely different from a stirred one, but both are damn tasty drinks.

2) A shaken Martini will be more aerated than a stirred Martini, and will appear cloudy when you first make it.

3) Shaking a Martini will never result in a Martini that is as cold as it's possible to get a stirred Martini.

4) A shaken Martini will (to my mind) need to be double-strained to remove shards of ice from the drink that result from shaking.

5) A stirred Martini gives you more control over the final drink, as you can check the dilution and temperature of the cocktail as you make it, whereas you have to trust your gut instinct on when to stop shaking and hope for the best – or practise lots until it becomes second nature.

6) A shaken Martini will be quicker to make than a stirred one, and you never know when this may come in handy!

Garnish

Finally, you need to decide how to garnish your Martini. Depending on the gin you've used you may want to use citrus, olives or take inspiration from one of the botanicals in the gin itself. Classically, a gin Martini is served with a lemon twist (as per the recipe below), spritzing the oils from the peel over the top of the drink before dropping it into the liquid. Beware on this point, though: too often a Martini is ruined with the addition of too much citrus oil from too large a piece of zest. The lemon oils are there to lift and freshen the cocktail, not to result in a drink that tastes of lemon and only lemon. For a standard 70–80ml Martini, a zest strip just bigger than your thumbnail is more than enough.

Martini variants

There are many different variants of the Martini aside from the gin-to-vermouth ratio. Some of the most common are:

- Dirty Martini – Add a bar spoon (approximately 5ml) of olive brine to the Martini, garnish with olives.
- Gibson Martini – Garnish your Martini with cocktail/ silverskin pickled onions.
- Burnt Martini – Rinse your cocktail glass with a smoky whisky before adding your Martini.

Ingredients   10ml vermouth
60ml gin

Method   Fill a mixing glass with ice, add the vermouth and stir to coat the ice. If at this point you want to make a drier Martini, you would strain out some of the vermouth and discard it. Add the gin and stir until chilled and diluted – you want to take some of the 'edge' off the neat gin. Strain into a chilled cocktail glass and garnish with a strip of lemon zest.

EL PRESIDENTE

The El Presidente cocktail was conceived during a time when America was going through Prohibition. Thirsty Americans unable to quench their thirst at home sailed to Havana from Florida to partake in a drink or two. Said to be named in honour of General Mario García Menocal y Deop, who later became president of Cuba, it then became the favourite of the country's next president, Gerardo Machado, to whom the drink is often (yet incorrectly) attributed.

It's a cocktail you'll see made slightly differently each time, the main issues being whether to add curaçao alongside the grenadine, and the ratios among the ingredients. The recipe below is the one that I prefer, and features slightly less curaçao than is often stated, allowing the rum to shine through alongside the vermouth.

Ingredients
60ml rum
30ml dry vermouth
10ml curaçao or triple sec
1 dash grenadine

Method
Fill a mixing glass with ice. Add all the ingredients and stir until chilled. Strain into a chilled cocktail glass and garnish with a strip of orange zest.

LOST STEPS

Rather than choosing a straight Martini twist with tequila, I've taken the opportunity to include a brilliant cocktail created by a relatively new bartender in London. It's a drink I have loved since the first time I sipped it, and one that I order time and time again in the growing number of London bars that choose to list it on their menus. It involves slightly more preparation compared to a lot of the cocktails listed in this book, and a couple of unusual ingredients, but trust me when I say it's worth the effort.

Created by Nico Piazza, the Lost Steps is a simple mix of just three ingredients, but is so much more than the sum of its parts. The cardamom cordial helps to soften the tequila and the Chartreuse Elixir Vegetal (not to be confused with regular green Chartreuse) adds depth and a slightly bitter note. The result is an elegant, very easy-to-drink cocktail, with a unique sweet yet savoury flavour that finishes with a distinctive peppery aftertaste. Any well-made, 100 per cent agave tequila will work in this drink; however, the original calls for *ocho blanco*, and should you choose to use this particular tequila you'll understand the reason why I'm so smitten by it.

Ingredients   50ml ocho blanco tequila
25ml cardamom cordial (recipe below)
1 dash Chartreuse Elixir Vegetal. Being the perfectionist he is, Nico specifies exactly 1.25ml; how precise you want to be is completely up to you...

Method   Fill a mixing glass with ice. Add all the ingredients and stir until chilled. Strain into a chilled cocktail glass and garnish with a small disc of lemon zest.

For the cardamom cordial

10g green cardamom pods
1 litre water
550g sugar
14.2g citric acid
5.4g tartaric acid

Method   Break the cardamom pods open. Put the water, sugar and cardamom pods into a saucepan placed over a medium heat, stir and cook for around 10 minutes to infuse the mixture with the cardamom flavour. Add the citric and tartaric acids and strain through a sieve. Store in a bottle and keep refrigerated (the mixture will stay fresh for 2–3 days; longer if you add a dash or two of tequila).

HARVARD

The Harvard cocktail is a tribute to the Manhattan, but featuring Cognac instead of American whiskey. First published in *Modern American Drinks* by George Kappeler in 1895, it is one of a series of cocktails named after American Ivy League colleges.

Modern Harvards, including the recipe below, tend to be heavier on the Cognac than the original; the ratio of Cognac to vermouth works on a sliding scale, which is open to interpretation and experimentation to determine your preferred recipe. The addition of soda water is unusual, and marks it as quite different from the Manhattan. While not essential, to be true to the original it should be included.

Ingredients

60ml Cognac
20ml sweet vermouth
2–3 dashes Angostura bitters
soda water

Method

Fill a mixing glass with ice. Add the Cognac, sweet vermouth and bitters and stir until chilled. Strain into a chilled cocktail glass. Top with around 50ml (a double shot) of soda water and garnish with a strip of orange zest.

RUM OLD-FASHIONED

The Old-fashioned is a cocktail made by combining sugar, bitters, spirit and citrus zest. It's one of the best ways to introduce a novice to any spirit's complexity and mixability, as the combination softens the spirit content while allowing its character to shine through. Given the limited ingredients, though, it's important to use a quality spirit as the base.

Some recipes list a maraschino cherry as the garnish; others take it one step further and prescribe muddling the cherry along with an orange wedge in the bottom of the glass before adding the spirit. The classic steers clear of both, and is a better cocktail for it, as the addition of cherry and/or orange juices from a wedge tends to over-sweeten the drink.

Whatever spirit you choose, there are two main ways of making an Old-fashioned. The recipe below uses rum to demonstrate this:

Ingredients   10ml sugar syrup (see Glossary, page 143) or a bar spoon
(long-handled mixing spoon) of sugar
2–3 dashes Angostura bitters
50ml golden or dark rum

Method #1   **(using sugar syrup)** Add a large disc of orange zest to the bottom of a rocks glass along with the sugar syrup, bitters and 25ml of the rum. Add two cubes of ice and stir 20–30 times to dilute. Add the remaining rum, two more ice cubes and stir again.

Method #2   **(using granulated sugar)** Put the sugar and the bitters into a rocks glass. Use a small amount of rum and stir with a spoon to dissolve the sugar. Add 25ml of the rum to the glass along with two cubes of ice and stir 20–30 times to dilute. Add a large disc of orange zest, the remaining rum, and two more ice cubes before stirring again.

MANHATTAN

The Manhattan belongs to a series of cocktails named after New York City's five boroughs, alongside cocktails such as the Bronx and the Brooklyn. Over the years it is the Manhattan that has become the most well known of these 'borough' cocktails; indeed, you'll be hard-stretched to find a bartender who doesn't know how to make one. The first written recipe for the Manhattan appeared in O.H. Byron's *The Modern Bartender's Guide*, published in 1884, which in fact contained two different versions. It is also one of six basic drinks listed in David A. Embury's classic, *The Fine Art of Mixing Drinks*, published in 1948.

Given the period when the original Manhattan was created, it would have used rye whiskey, a lighter style of whiskey than the now more commonly used bourbon, Canadian whisky, blended or Tennessee whiskies. So long as you use a good-quality spirit, all of these variants will make a decent cocktail, but given the recent resurgence of rye and the number of examples that are now easy enough to get hold of, I'd highly recommend trying a rye version.

As with many classic cocktails of the Manhattan era, there are a number of ways you can order or serve a Manhattan cocktail. You can take one sweet, dry or 'perfect', which refers to the type of vermouth used in the final cocktail.

A classic Manhattan uses sweet vermouth, but this can be called a sweet Manhattan (to avoid confusion when ordering). A dry Manhattan uses dry vermouth (sometimes switching out the cherry garnish for a lemon twist), and a perfect Manhattan uses a 50:50 ratio of sweet and dry vermouths.

Traditionally the bitters used in the Manhattan would have been Angostura, but some champion the use of other bitters such as Abbott's, so feel free to play around. Some modern formulations of the sweet Manhattan also suggest adding a little of the syrup from the maraschino cherry to the cocktail. American whiskies and maraschino are very well matched, so it's understandable how and why this has come about; however, I would recommend being careful with how much of the syrup you add if you decide to try this addition, as you don't want to overly sweeten what is already quite a sweet mix.

Ingredients

60ml American whiskey: bourbon or rye
20ml vermouth (dry, sweet or a 50:50 mixture of both, depending on the preference)
2–3 dashes bitters (generally less in a dry Manhattan)

Method

Fill a mixing glass with ice. Add all of the ingredients and stir until chilled. Strain into a chilled cocktail glass and garnish with a maraschino cherry (sweet/perfect) or a strip of lemon zest (dry).

10   3
Rr
Rob Roy

ROB ROY

The Rob Roy is simply a Manhattan served with Scotch whisky. Unlike the Manhattan, though, it's usually served sweet (as in using sweet vermouth exclusively), although you can try one dry or perfect and make up your own mind.

As it's generally mixed with a sweet vermouth, I'd recommend using a blended rather than a single-malt Scotch, as the addition of sweet vermouth means you're unlikely to be able to discern the specific nuances of the single malt, and blends have the advantage of generally being cheaper.

Created at the Waldorf Astoria Hotel in New York in 1894, this cocktail is said to be named after Robert Roy MacGregor, a Scottish hero and outlaw whose story was being immortalised in a play on Broadway at the time.

Ingredients   60ml Scotch whisky
20ml sweet vermouth
2–3 dashes Angostura bitters

Method   Fill a mixing glass with ice. Add all of the ingredients and stir until chilled. Strain into a chilled cocktail glass and garnish with a maraschino cherry.

Daisies,
sours and
citrus fresh

The cocktails within the next few columns occupy what is termed the 'transition metals' in the classic periodic table. As with the original element table, I have grouped these together into a cohesive section rather than define each column separately.

The cocktails in this group tend to be more citrus-led, or slightly longer drinks than those found in the first column. They then evolve as you move right across the group, to include more citrus, egg white, liqueur and syrup/liqueur-based sweetening agents (rather than the traditional vermouths), and finally juices such as cranberry and orange.

There are two classic families of cocktails that feature heavily in this grouping and chapter: daisies and sours.

A sour consists of a base spirit, citrus, a sweetening agent of some sort and optional egg white (in my mind this isn't optional at all, but completely necessary!). These combine to make a cocktail that is wonderfully balanced, with a silky, creamy texture.

When making a cocktail with egg white it's recommended to shake the mixture without ice first (termed a dry shake) to emulsify the egg white, making sure that the ingredients are thoroughly mixed and starting to froth up. An insider secret: if you're using a cocktail strainer with a metal spring around its edge (aka a Hawthorne strainer), take the spring off and pop it in the shaker; it will act a little like a whisk and help the foam to develop. Or, if you've got one of those battery-powered milk frothers that you get in hot-chocolate gift packs, a quick blast with that will do the trick. Then add ice and shake normally (termed a wet shake) before straining over ice.

The daisy family of cocktails was popular in the early 20th century. They contain spirit, citrus juice and a sweetening agent. Not altogether dissimilar to a sour, you say? Not at all; you just don't add the egg white. Famous examples include the Margarita (coincidently the Spanish word for daisy), and the Daiquiri.

Column 2

1 Hp Hanky Panky [3]		
2 Mz Martinez [5]		
3 V Vesper [3]		
4 Ma Martini [2]	11 Av Aviation [4]	18 Dd Dill or No Dill [6]
5 Ep El Presidente [4]	12 Da Daiquiri [3]	19 Mc Maid in Cuba [7]
6 Ls Lost Steps [3]	13 Mr Margarita [3]	20 Mt Matador [3]
7 H Havard [4]	14 By Brandy Daisy [6]	21 Si Sidecar [3]
8 Ro Rum Old-fashioned [3]	15 Tr Treacle [4]	22 Jb Jungle Bird [5]
9 Mn Manhattan [3]	16 Br Brooklyn [4]	23 Sf Scofflaw [4]
10 Rr Rob Roy [3]	17 Bb Bobby Burns [3]	24 Pe Penicillin [4]

AVIATION

The first published recipe for an Aviation appeared in 1916 in Hugo R. Ensslin's *Recipes for Mixed Drinks*. A mixture of gin, lemon juice, maraschino liqueur and crème de violette – a violet liqueur that gives it a naturally light-blue colour – the proportions specified make for quite a sour drink. The cocktail also features in Harry Craddock's *The Savoy Cocktail Book*, published in 1930; however, Craddock omits the crème de violette, probably because the liqueur was difficult to get hold of at the time, both in Europe and the States – or maybe it was a typo. Who knows?

There has been discussion ever since as to whether to include the violette, and debate over the proportions of the other ingredients. For me, an Aviation without the violette isn't quite right – there's something missing, and the final drink doesn't have the wonderful light-blue/purple colour you'd expect from a cocktail named after attempts to conquer the skies. To my mind, therefore, there is no question: violette *must* be added.

In terms of the proportions of the other ingredients, while the Aviation is unquestionably a twist on a gin sour, the amount of lemon juice included in the classic recipes mentioned above throws the balance of the cocktail off (for me, at least). The quantities specified below have therefore been adjusted to result in a cocktail that is both easy to drink and classically blue. Let's face it: who doesn't (perhaps secretly) love a blue drink?

Ingredients

50ml gin
25ml lemon juice
15ml maraschino liqueur
5–10ml crème de violette (depending on the brand you use; some are more potent than others)

Method

Add all the ingredients to a cocktail shaker. Shake over ice and double-strain into a chilled Martini glass or Champagne coupe. Garnish with a maraschino cherry.

DAIQUIRI

The Daiquiri is a very simple combination of rum, lime and sugar. The name actually refers to a family of cocktails, which includes any that follows the formula above; however, most people will expect to be served the classic when they order a Daiquiri at the bar.

The creation of the Daiquiri is attributed to the American engineer Jennings Stockton Cox, who worked in the Daiquiri mine in southeast Cuba in the 1890s. Insisting on a monthly rum ration for his engineers, he was said to have come up with the Daiquiri, containing rum, citrus and sugar, when entertaining guests. The cocktail was then named after the mine. Unlike many classic cocktails of this age, the history and origin of the Daiquiri is well recorded, both in Cox's personal diary and in a 1928 cocktail book, *When It's Cocktail Time in Cuba*, written by Basil Woon, where the story is recounted. The original recipe calls for lemon, but this is likely to have been an error in translation, as the Cuban term for lime is *limón*, and limes are native to Cuba (whereas lemons are not). All of that said, it is likely that the mix of the local spirit (rum), the local citrus (lime) along with something to sweeten, had been drunk for years before this. The story is instead a history of how it came to be known as the Daiquiri.

The cocktail became well known in America during wartime in 1940. Whereas other spirits such as whisky and gin from the UK, or vodka from Eastern Europe, became difficult to get hold of, the Good Neighbor Policy introduced by Franklin D. Roosevelt brought in goods from Latin America, Cuba and the Caribbean, making rum widely available in the States. It has remained popular ever since.

The Daiquiri 'formula' hasn't changed over the years – after all, why mess with a formula that works so well? It was considered alongside another five drinks as key 'basic' drinks to know by David A. Embury in his 1948 publication, *The Fine Art of Mixing Drinks*.

Ingredients
50ml white rum
20ml lime juice
15ml sugar syrup (see Glossary, page 143)

Method
Add all the ingredients to a cocktail shaker. Shake hard over ice until well diluted (Embury prescribed shaking with crushed ice to ensure enough dilution). Double-strain into a chilled Martini glass or Champagne coupe. Classically the Daiquiri is garnished with a lime wedge on the rim of the glass, although if you're a fan of the 90s school of thinking, why not go for a whole lime wheel?

MARGARITA

As with many cocktails, it depends on whether you're looking for the name of the drink or the combination of ingredients. A Margarita is arguably a tequila Sidecar of sorts (granted, with lime juice rather than lemon juice) or a tequila daisy. There is also a cocktail in the iconic *Café Royal Cocktail Book* by W. J. Tarling (1937) called a Picador, which lists tequila, Cointreau and lime juice as ingredients. The first mention of the well-known ingredients in a Margarita that is named as such is in a 1953 edition of *Esquire* magazine, which called for either lime or lemon juice. Was the cocktail eventually named after a woman? Most would like to think so; after all, it makes a great story. Or was it created by a bartender in Tijuana? What is likely is that the influx of Americans to Mexico during Prohibition brought their taste for cocktails with them.

The key to making a great Margarita is using fresh lime juice, squeezed by hand just before it's needed. To get the most juice out of the fruit, store limes at room temperature and roll them gently along a flat surface before squeezing.

Ingredients
50ml tequila
30ml lime juice
25ml triple sec or curaçao

Method   Shake all the ingredients with ice and double-strain into a
               Martini glass with a salted rim. Garnish with a lime wheel
               or wedge on the side of the glass.

Tommy's Margarita

The most famous twist on a Margarita is unquestionably
the Tommy's Margarita. Created by tequila legend Julio
Bermejo at Tommy's restaurant in San Francisco, the now-
iconic Tommy's Margarita features agave syrup in place
of the curaçao, and it is served on the rocks with no salt.

Ingredients   50ml tequila
                    30ml lime juice
                    25ml agave syrup*

                    *make a 50:50 mixture of agave syrup and water

Method   Shake all the ingredients with ice in a cocktail shaker and
               strain into a rocks glass filled with ice. Garnish with a
               lime wheel.

BRANDY DAISY

Daisies belong to one of the older cocktail families,
alongside crustas and fixes. Created in the mid-19th
century, the Daisy formula involves spirit, citrus,
sweetening agent and a dash of soda or seltzer. Sounds
like quite a lot of cocktails, doesn't it? You're right. As
with these old families and styles of cocktails, there
is quite a lot of variation as to what ingredients to use
(alcoholic liqueur as the sweetener or a non-alcoholic
syrup or cordial?), the type of ice (shaved? cracked?
crushed? cubed?) and how you serve it (in a wine glass
or goblet or a highball glass?). After much research I
think it's almost impossible to get to the bottom of these
questions. Therefore, the recipe below is the one that I
make, and it's both delicious and accessible.

The Brandy Daisy is perhaps the 'original' daisy, at least
where base spirit is concerned. One of the earliest recipes
is from 1862, in *Jerry Thomas' Bartenders Guide or How*

To Mix Drinks: The Bon Vivant's Companion. It calls for gum syrup (sugar syrup with gum arabic added), orange-flavoured liqueur, lemon, brandy and a couple of dashes of rum. Later the 'formula' would be applied to all kinds of spirits, resulting in the Gin Daisy, or even the Whisky Daisy.

Ingredients   50ml Cognac
10ml triple sec or curaçao
20ml lemon juice
5ml sugar syrup (see Glossary, page 143)
soda water
2 dashes Jamaican rum

Method   Add the Cognac, triple sec, lemon juice and sugar syrup to a cocktail shaker. Fill with ice and shake well. Strain into a large wine glass or julep cup filled with ice. Top up with a little soda water (be careful not to over-dilute your cocktail; you can always add a little more later) and finish with a couple of dashes of Jamaican rum over the top. Garnish with seasonal fruits – redcurrants and blackberries look especially lovely if they're in season – and a sprig of mint for freshness. Some bars like to dust a little icing sugar over the top, especially if serving in a julep cup, for aesthetic reasons.

TREACLE

The Treacle is a simple yet brilliant twist on an Old-fashioned, made with rum and with the addition of apple juice. The key is to use a Jamaican rum, which gives an aromatic and rich flavour to the cocktail, and pressed apple juice if possible. A modern classic created by London bartender Dick Bradsell, a name that you'll see mentioned a couple of times in this book. It follows his formula of simple ingredients, matched due to their flavours and balanced perfectly.

Ingredients   10ml sugar syrup (see Glossary, page 143)
2 dashes Angostura bitters
50ml Jamaican rum
15ml apple juice

Method   Add the sugar syrup, bitters, half the rum and two ice cubes to a rocks glass. Stir. Add the remaining rum, another couple of ice cubes, and stir again. Fill the glass with ice and float the apple juice on top. Garnish with a strip of lemon zest.

BROOKLYN

Amer Picon is a bittersweet French apéritif dating back to 1837 with a dominant orange flavour. The key to this drink is to balance the spiciness from the rye with the bitterness from the Amer Picon and the sweetness from the maraschino, using the dry vermouth to bring them all together. While there are many different recipes out there for the Brooklyn, the ratios below work perfectly and are taken from Ted Haigh's *Vintage Spirits and Forgotten Cocktails* (2009).

Ingredients   60ml rye whiskey
30ml dry vermouth
10ml Amer Picon
10ml maraschino liqueur

Method   Fill a mixing glass with ice. Add all of the ingredients and stir until chilled. Strain into a chilled cocktail glass and garnish with a maraschino cherry.

BOBBY BURNS

Named after Scottish poet Robert Burns, the Bobby Burns was first featured in print in Harry Craddock's *The Savoy Cocktail Book* (1930). A version of the cocktail features in David A. Embury's *The Fine Art of Mixing Drinks* (1948); however, Embury's version substitutes the Benedictine used in Craddock's for Drambuie. Both versions are delicious in their own ways; Benedictine adds more herbal elements, whereas Drambuie adds sweeter notes. As I don't have a sweet tooth, I tend to go with Benedictine, but do try both and decide for yourself!

Classic recipes call for equal proportions of Scotch and vermouth, but the heavy vermouth tends to result in a cocktail that's a tad too sweet for modern palates. Modern Bobby Burns recipes therefore tend to prescribe a 2:1 ratio (as below).

Ingredients

60ml Scotch whisky
30ml sweet vermouth
3 dashes Benedictine or Drambuie

Method

Fill a mixing glass with ice. Add all of the ingredients and stir until chilled. Strain into a chilled cocktail glass and garnish with a strip of lemon zest.

Column 3

11 4 **Av** Aviation	18 6 **Dd** Dill or No Dill	25 4 **Wl** White Lady
12 3 **Da** Daiquiri	19 7 **Mc** Maid in Cuba	26 4 **Bs** Between the Sheets
13 3 **Mr** Margarita	20 3 **Mt** Matador	27 4 **Ts** Tequila Sour
14 6 **By** Brandy Daisy	21 3 **Si** Sidecar	28 6 **Bc** Brandy Crusta
15 4 **Tr** Treacle	22 5 **Jb** Jungle Bird	29 6 **Mi** Mai Tai
16 4 **Br** Brooklyn	23 4 **Sf** Scofflaw	30 5 **Ws** Whisky Sour
17 3 **Bb** Bobby Burns	24 4 **Pe** Penicillin	31 5 **Ns** New York Sour

DILL OR NO DILL

Created by London bartender Gareth Evans for the 2013 round of the Diageo World Class competition, the amusingly named 'Dill or No Dill' helped him reach the world finals. A beautifully fresh combination, the addition of smoked sea salt helps to soften the acidity from the lemon juice without needing to add excess sweetening agents (in this case, more elderflower cordial, which would cause the elderflower flavour to overpower the drink). If you can't get hold of cucumber water, muddle a couple of slices of cucumber in the bottom of the cocktail shaker before adding the other ingredients.

Ingredients
50ml gin
30ml cucumber water
15ml elderflower cordial
10ml lemon juice
2 sprigs dill
pinch smoked sea salt

Method
Add all the ingredients to a cocktail shaker. Shake hard over ice to ensure the dill is well incorporated into the liquid, and then double-strain into a chilled Martini glass or Champagne coupe. Garnish with a sprig of dill.

MAID IN CUBA

The Maid in Cuba was created by British bartender Tom Walker for the 2014 Bacardi Legacy cocktail competition. Inspired by the maid style of cocktail, which traditionally consists of a spirit mixed with lime juice, mint and cucumber, Tom found that there wasn't an example using rum.

Given the similarity in flavour profile to the classic Daiquiri, rum proved a successful addition to the maid style. The resulting cocktail, called the Maid in Cuba, benefits from the freshness of the mint and cucumber, and the slightly herbal edge provided by the absinthe. It's not surprising that Tom went on to win the 2014 competition at the finals in Russia with this brilliant cocktail, and thanks to the fact that part of the competition involves promoting your cocktail around the world, it's well on its way to becoming a modern classic.

Ingredients
1 dash absinthe
4 slices cucumber (reserve one for garnishing)
6 mint leaves
15ml sugar syrup (2:1; see Glossary, page 143)
30ml lime juice
60ml white rum
50ml soda water

Method
Pour the absinthe into an ice-filled cocktail glass. Top with cold tap water and leave to stand. Add the cucumber, mint, sugar syrup and lime juice to a shaker. Bruise gently. Add the rum. Add ice and shake.

Empty the cocktail glass and then double-strain the mix from the shaker into the cocktail glass. Top up with soda. Garnish with a slice of cucumber.

To stay true to the original recipe, Bacardi Superior white rum should be used; however, other white rums will also work. Tom also created his own 'sweet-and-sour mix' by adding the sugar syrup and lime juice together and leaving them to infuse for half a day. The recipe above works a treat, but if you have time for some extra preparation, why not try the infusion method?

MATADOR

The recipe for a Matador was included in Trader Vic's *Bartender's Guide*, published in 1947. It's similar to the classic Margarita, but instead of the usual triple sec it features pineapple juice. The amount of pineapple juice needs to be adequate enough to balance the citrus lime juice, but you may find that you need to increase the amount of tequila to suit modern palates. Freshly pressed pineapple juice works best, both for flavour and colour: you're looking for a fresh, citrussy cocktail with a yellow glow rather than a muddy orange colour.

Ingredients	30ml blanco tequila 20ml lime juice 60ml pineapple juice
Method	Add all the ingredients to a cocktail shaker. Shake hard over ice to ensure that the pineapple juice is well mixed (it will create a smooth texture and a foam to develop on top of the drink). Double-strain into a chilled Martini glass or Champagne coupe. Garnish with a lime or pineapple wedge.

21 3

Si

Sidecar

SIDECAR

The Sidecar is a mix of Cognac (though you can use any quality brandy), triple sec and lemon juice. Properly made, it is a wonderfully well-balanced and dangerously drinkable cocktail. It is almost identical to the Brandy Crusta, found in Jerry Thomas' 1862 book, *Bartenders Guide or How to Mix Drinks or The Bon Vivant's Companion*, which only differs in the addition of bitters; however, the true origin of the cocktail now known as the Sidecar is disputed. Some swear by a great story featuring an American army captain who walked into Harry's New York Bar in Paris in 1920 and maintain the cocktail was named after the sidecar from the motorcycle he drove; others say it was invented in New Orleans and often touted as the only good cocktail to come out of Prohibition, where bartenders named it after the term they use for leftover liquor they pour into shot glasses (hardly a tale to get your mouth watering, though, is it?). What is known is that the first recipes for the Sidecar appear in print in Harry MacElhone's *Harry's ABC of Mixing Cocktails* (1919) and Robert Vermeire's *Cocktails: How to Mix Them* (1922).

Along with its origin, there is also discussion as to the ratios of the 'perfect' Sidecar, ranging from equal amounts of each of the ingredients, to 2:1:1 listed opposite and prescribed in Harry Craddock's *The Savoy Cocktail Book* (1930), and 8:2:1 recommended by David A. Embury in *The Fine Art of Mixing Drinks* (1948).

While I follow Craddock's ratios, don't be afraid to play around with the proportions of each ingredient to find your preferred recipe. Just remember the principle of balancing the sweet and sour elements.

Traditionally, the Sidecar is served in a sugar-rimmed glass. In my opinion it's unnecessary, but if you do include it I strongly recommend including a strip of lemon zest too, as the oils expressed from the peel help to lift the cocktail, and work to balance the extra sweetness from the sugar rim. You may also want to reduce the amount of triple sec slightly.

Ingredients   50ml Cognac or brandy
25ml triple sec
25ml lemon juice

Method   Add all the ingredients to a cocktail shaker. Shake hard over ice and double-strain into a chilled Martini glass or Champagne coupe. Garnish with a strip of lemon zest and optional sugar rim.

JUNGLE BIRD

The Jungle Bird is a classic tiki drink (see Glossary, page 143), invented at the Aviary Bar at the Hilton Hotel in Kuala Lumpur. The addition of Campari does mean it's quite unusual in terms of tiki cocktails; however, it's not as bitter as you might expect, given the inclusion of the well-known apéritif.

The dark rum specifically called for in the Jungle Bird is Cruzan Black Strap Rum, which is made in the navy-rum style and is rich in flavour, yet slightly lighter than other dark rums in the category. However, most well-made dark rums will make a good-quality Jungle Bird.

Ingredients   45ml dark rum
20ml Campari
15ml lime juice
15ml sugar syrup (see Glossary, page 143)
45ml pineapple juice

Method   Add all the ingredients to a cocktail shaker. Shake hard over ice and strain into a rocks glass filled with crushed ice. Garnish with anything tiki: an orange slice, pineapple wedge or leaf, mint sprig, maraschino cherry – or the lot!

SCOFFLAW

The word 'scofflaw', like the cocktail, was created during Prohibition in the US. A scofflaw was 'a lawless drinker of illegally made or illegally obtained liquor'. Unusually, the origin of the word is well documented, as it was the result of a competition run by *The Boston Herald*, which was designed to shame those Americans still drinking during the ban.

According to *Barflies and Cocktails* by Harry MacElhone (1927), the cocktail of the same name came into being just 12 days after the term was coined. 'Jock', a bartender from Harry's American Bar in Paris, created the drink to 'celebrate' the new term as the rest of the world continued to be baffled and amused at the idea of Prohibition in the States.

The key to the Scofflaw is to make sure that you use a good-quality grenadine. Why not make your own at home (see recipe below)?

Ingredients   45ml rye whiskey
25ml dry vermouth
20ml lemon juice
20ml grenadine

Method   Add all the ingredients to a cocktail shaker. Add ice and shake well. Double-strain into a chilled Martini glass or Champagne coupe. Garnish with a twist of lemon peel.

To make grenadine

Combine equal amounts of pomegranate juice (fresh from the fruit or in a carton but it MUST be unsweetened) and sugar in a bottle or airtight jar and shake vigorously until the sugar has dissolved. Some recipes also call for orange-blossom water or rose water to taste; whether you add these is completely up to you, but be careful if you opt for rose water as it's a powerful flavour. Add a shot (25ml) or so of vodka to help preserve the grenadine – but only if using it for boozy cocktails – and it will last for three to four weeks in the fridge.

PENICILLIN

The Penicillin is a modern classic cocktail, created in 2005 by Sam Ross in Milk and Honey on Manhattan's Lower East Side. Word spread of the simple yet delicious combination, and it is now listed on menus in countless bars around the world.

The name is a joke about the idea that this delicious drink is sure to cure any ill. The name is also short yet recognisable, the ingredient list short and familiar, and the combination is delicious: all important factors in allowing a cocktail to transition into the realm of 'modern classic'.

The recipe calls for two types of Scotch. The first can be any single malt or blend, but the recipe works best with a whisky that is slightly peated. The key is the addition of the second whisky – just 10ml – which should be a heavily peated Islay. My preference? Laphroaig.

The result is a drink that gives a fiery kick of ginger to begin with, citrus and Scotch in the middle, and ends with a smoky, peaty finish, thanks to the Islay whisky.

Ingredients
60ml single-malt or blended Scotch whisky
10ml Islay whisky
30ml lemon juice
30ml honey-ginger syrup (recipe on page 38)

Method
Add all the ingredients to a cocktail shaker*. Shake hard over ice and strain into a rocks glass, preferably with one large ice cube or ice ball; otherwise filled with cubed ice. Garnish with candied ginger if you can get your hands on some.

*Some advise floating the Islay whisky on top of the drink. Granted, it makes the peat notes much more evident on the nose, but I prefer to shake all of the ingredients together.

For the honey-ginger syrup

100ml honey
100ml water
25–30g fresh root ginger (peeled and sliced)

Method   Add all the ingredients to a saucepan. Bring to the boil
and simmer for 10 minutes. Allow to cool, then strain to
remove the pieces of ginger. Store in the fridge (it will
keep for around a week; longer if you add a couple of
dashes of something boozy: vodka, whisky, etc).

Column 4

18 6 **Dd** Dill or No Dill	25 4 **Wl** White Lady	32 4 **Bk** Breakfast Martini
19 7 **Mc** Maid in Cuba	26 4 **Bs** Between the Sheets	33 4 **Hd** Hemingway Daiquiri
20 3 **Mt** Matador	27 4 **Ts** Tequila Sour	34 4 **Rc** Rude Cosmopolitan
21 3 **Si** Sidecar	28 6 **Bc** Brandy Crusta	35 4 **Su** Sundowner
22 5 **Jb** Jungle Bird	29 6 **Mi** Mai Tai	36 4 **Pk** Painkiller
23 4 **Sf** Scofflaw	30 5 **Ws** Whisky Sour	37 5 **Kr** King of Roses
24 4 **Pe** Penicillin	31 5 **Ns** New York Sour	38 4 **Bl** Blood and Sand

25   4
WI
White Lady

WHITE LADY

There are two differing opinions on who created the White Lady. The first story features Harry MacElhone, who worked in London in the 1920s. He originally used lemon juice, triple sec and crème de menthe (equal amounts of each), before replacing the latter with gin in 1929, at the bar he became synonymous with, Harry's New York Bar in Paris. However, Harry Craddock also lays claim to the White Lady, claiming it for his own. A recipe for a White Lady cocktail featuring gin, Cointreau and fresh lemon juice appears in Craddock's *The Savoy Cocktail Book*, which was published in 1930.

Neither recipe calls for egg white, although it is generally included by all bartenders today for two good reasons. Firstly, the addition of the egg white helps to bind the flavours together, and gives a silky mouthfeel and texture to the drink. Secondly, it also makes the drink white – well, at least the foam on top is. Without the addition of egg white, depending on the triple sec you use, the drink will have a yellow-orange colour (for this reason I suggest using a clear liqueur if possible).

Depending on the triple sec (many have become drier over the years), you may want to add a touch of sugar syrup (see Glossary, page 143) to balance the citrus acidity from the lemon juice. This is preferable to using less lemon, as the White Lady should be a citrus-led cocktail.

Ingredients   50ml gin
20ml lemon juice
20m triple sec
egg white (optional)

Method   Add all the ingredients to a cocktail shaker. Shake without ice, then add ice and shake again. Strain into a chilled Martini glass or Champagne coupe. Garnish with a strip of lemon peel.

BETWEEN THE SHEETS

Dating back to Prohibition, the Between the Sheets cocktail is a little unusual in that it mixes two different spirits (most cocktails feature a single spirit alongside liqueurs, vermouths, etc). Created by Harry MacElhone of Harry's New York Bar in Paris, it is therefore stronger than the closely-related Sidecar, yet when made properly, it is a well-balanced and smooth libation.

Ingredients   20ml white rum
20ml Cognac
20ml Cointreau
10ml lemon juice

Method   Add all the ingredients to a cocktail shaker. Add ice and shake well. Double-strain into a chilled Martini glass or Champagne coupe. Garnish with a strip of twisted lemon zest.

TEQUILA SOUR

A standard sour formula made with tequila. You can use any type of tequila, from an unaged *blanco* through to a mature *añejo*. Personally I like the freshness of a *blanco*, especially alongside freshly squeezed lime juice.

The key to making a sour is to make sure that the cocktail is shaken really well. A double shake will aid the emulsification of the egg white (egg white, to my mind, is crucial to a sour as it gives a wonderfully smooth and creamy texture); however, your second shake with ice (sometimes termed wet shake) is equally important, as this dilutes and chills the drink.

Ingredients   50ml tequila
25ml lime juice
20ml sugar syrup (see Glossary, page 143)
egg white

Method   Add all the ingredients to a cocktail shaker. Shake without ice (dry shake), then add ice and shake again (wet shake). Strain into a rocks glass over ice.

BRANDY CRUSTA

Created in 1852 by Joseph Santina at Jewel of the South in New Orleans, the name refers to the crust of sugar around the rim. The first printed recipe is in *Jerry Thomas' Bartenders Guide or How To Mix Drinks: The Bon Vivant's Companion* from 1862, calling for Boker's Bitters (the recipe of which has been reformulated by Dr Adam Elmegirab). It's a precursor to the Sidecar, which most likely evolved due to the crusta's garnish being quite elaborate.

The garnish for a Crusta is also unique, as it is one of very few cocktails where you attend to it before the drink itself. The best method I've come up with is below, but you'll find quite a few different ways of achieving the same effect, depending on your preferences level of knife skills and how much time you have.

Ingredients
50ml Cognac
20ml lemon juice
5ml triple sec
5ml maraschino liqueur
1–2 dashes sugar syrup (see Glossary, page 143)
2 dashes Boker's Bitters

Method
Prepare your garnish: find a lemon that fits snugly into the top of the glass you intend to use, and cut a thick wheel around 3cm thick from the middle. Hollow out the middle, removing all of the flesh and the majority of the pith. Place into the glass with around 1cm of peel above the rim (this is why it's important that the lemon peel fits well into the glass). Dip the top of the peel and the glass into some lemon juice, then into sugar to create a sugar rim. If you leave this for a couple of hours you'll be left with a pretty hard crust of sugar around the rim, which has the advantage of not sweetening your drink too much when you come to drink it; however, it also makes it a little more difficult to clean!

Add all the ingredients to a cocktail shaker. Shake hard over ice and double-strain into the prepared glass.

MAI TAI

Named after the Tahitian phrase for 'amazing' or 'out of this world' – *Maita'i roa ae!* – the Mai Tai (separated into two words because it was easier to read, pronounce and recognise), is another cocktail with disputed origins. I, however, have it on good authority from rum enthusiast Peter Holland of TheFloatingRumShack.com, that Trader Vic's 1944 version is the ONLY version worthy of the name. And who's to argue when the result is so damn delicious?

Vic takes the Daiquiri template and twists it. With a rum-and-lime-juice base (choosing one with a good depth of flavour is important), the Mai Tai then includes sweet components of sugar syrup and orgeat syrup. There should be a healthy dollop of orgeat syrup in the mix, so feel free to up the volume of orgeat syrup (and reduce the sugar syrup) if you'd like – you'll get no objections from me – or from Mr Holland for that matter.

Putting all arguments aside as to who created the cocktail originally, what's clear is that the Mai Tai is definitely *not* a fruit-juice-based cocktail (as is so frequently assumed). Instead, it's a strong, rum-based tiki-style drink (see Glossary, page 143). Any version with grenadine and pineapple juice isn't what you're looking for. Oh, and never use a white rum – always choose gold or dark. Trader Vic championed the use of Wray & Nephew 17-year-old; however, it ceased to be produced and therefore had to be substituted. So don't be afraid to experiment with different types of rum, or blending your own mix for your Mai Tais. Just make sure that you use strong, bold-flavoured rum to balance the orgeat syrup.

The garnish is often described as 'Sink your spent lime shell in the drink and garnish with a big sprig of mint'. Subsequently, the half-shell had the mint sprig pushed through it to resemble a palm tree on a desert island. As with all things tiki, whatever you use to garnish the cocktail, it should be fun!

Ingredients   30ml Jamaican rum
30ml agricole rum
30ml lime juice
15ml curaçao
10ml orgeat syrup
10ml sugar syrup (see Glossary, page 143)

Method   Add all the ingredients to a cocktail shaker. Add crushed
or cracked ice and shake well. Strain into a rocks glass
filled with ice and garnish with half of the 'spent' lime and
a mint sprig.

THE WHISKY SOUR AND
THE NEW YORK SOUR

These two drinks are remarkably similar, yet the simple
addition of a red-wine float to the New York Sour
changes the drink, not only aesthetically, but also by
adding a depth and fruity element to it. It's one of the
simplest yet most effective twists on a cocktail I have
encountered.

I like to add the bitters to the top of a Whisky Sour
The key to both drinks is to make sure that your mix
of whisky/bourbon/rye (depending on your preference),
lemon juice, egg white and sugar syrup is shaken really
well. A double shake will aid the emulsification of the
egg white (egg white, to my mind, is crucial to a sour
as it gives a wonderfully smooth and creamy texture).
However, your second shake with ice (sometimes termed
a wet shake) is equally important, as this will dilute and
chill the drink.

I like to add the bitters to the top of a Whisky Sour
after shaking, because then you get a lovely light-yellow
hue to the drink (bitters can turn it a little murky if you
shake with them), and they also create colour through
the foam on top as they fall through into the drink if you
add them afterwards. You will find that some bartenders
take advantage of this to create patterns in the foam.
To have a go yourself, drip the bitters carefully through
the foam in four or five places around the edge of the

drink, creating small circles of colour, then trace a line through each using a toothpick to drag the colour through the foam.

In terms of the New York Sour, you can either serve it over ice or straight up in a cocktail glass. Personally I always serve over ice. Any reasonable-quality red wine will do; there's no need to raid the fancy dusty bottles in the cellar or head to the shop to buy something super-expensive. Fruity reds like Merlot or Malbec generally work well – basically anything with blackberry or berry notes.

The idea is to float the wine on the top of the shaken portion of the drink, so be sure to pour the wine slowly and carefully, although the temperature difference between the wine and the shaken whisky will make floating the wine easier.

Ingredients
60ml whisky, bourbon or rye
25ml lemon juice
20ml sugar syrup (see Glossary, page 143)
egg white
2–3 dashes Angostura bitters (omit for the New York Sour)
red wine float (omit for the Whisky Sour)

Method
Add the whisky, lemon juice, sugar syrup and egg white to a cocktail shaker. Shake without ice (dry shake), then add ice and shake again (wet shake). Strain into a rocks glass over ice (traditionally) and add the bitters (Whisky Sour) or red-wine float (New York Sour).

Column 5

25 — 4 **Wl** White Lady	32 — 4 **Bk** Breakfast Martini	39 — 8 **Ss** Singapore Sling
26 — 4 **Bs** Between the Sheets	33 — 4 **Hd** Hemingway Daiquiri	40 — 6 **Hu** Hurricane
27 — 4 **Ts** Tequila Sour	34 — 4 **Rc** Rude Cosmopolitan	41 — 3 **Te** Tequila Sunrise
28 — 6 **Bc** Brandy Crusta	35 — 4 **Su** Sundowner	42 — 5 **Fh** Fish House Punch
29 — 6 **Mi** Mai Tai	36 — 4 **Pk** Painkiller	43 — 3 **Pp** Planter's Punch
30 — 5 **Ws** Whisky Sour	37 — 5 **Kr** King of Roses	44 — 5 **Bu** Bourbon Smash
31 — 5 **Ns** New York Sour	38 — 4 **Bl** Blood and Sand	45 — 3 **Al** Algonquin

BREAKFAST MARTINI

Created by Salvatore Calabrese sometime in the late 1990s–early 2000s at the Library Bar in the Lanesborough Hotel in London, the Breakfast Martini is a jammy twist on a gin sour or White Lady. The marmalade adds texture to the drink, and it's worth spending a couple of extra pennies on the brand to ensure it's a well-made marmalade with a bittersweet flavour (I find cheap marmalades generally too heavy on the sugar).

The Breakfast Martini is quite similar to a cocktail featured in Harry Craddock's 1930s *The Savoy Cocktail Book* called the Marmalade Cocktail. However, Salvatore insists that the inspiration for the drink was breakfast with his wife and a simple way to twist the classic White Lady cocktail.

A refreshing drink that benefits from a citrus-led London Dry style of gin (in my opinion) which sits well with the Cointreau and the rich and slightly bitter edge of the marmalade. It's a dangerously drinkable cocktail, and one that is very well suited to being the first drink of the day, whether that be at breakfast, brunch or lunch.

While the classic lists a strip of orange zest as the garnish, many bars have decided to include a small triangle of toast with marmalade on the side of the cocktail as a play on the name. Why not?

Ingredients   50ml gin
15ml Cointreau
15ml lemon juice
1 bar spoon or teaspoon orange marmalade

Method   Add all the ingredients to a cocktail shaker. Shake hard over ice and double-strain into a chilled Martini glass or Champagne coupe. Garnish with a strip of orange zest – or a small slice of toast if you're so inclined!

HEMINGWAY DAIQUIRI

Ernest Hemingway loved a drink – that much is indisputable. However, a little-known fact is that he suffered from haemochromatosis, an inherited disorder in which a person absorbs too much iron from food. This excess iron then builds up in the body, and can cause issues for tissues and organs, including the heart, liver, pancreas and skin. Sufferers have to be very careful in their diet, which includes avoiding too much alcohol, due to effects on the liver; sugar, due to effects on the pancreas; and vitamin C, as it increases the amount of iron absorbed from food. Hemingway clearly ignored the majority of these instructions, particularly the alcohol aspect. However, he seemed to try to heed the sugar warning, at least as far as the story of the Hemingway Daiquiri would have you believe.

Hemingway lived in Havana, Cuba, during the 1920s and 1930s. During this time he drank at a bar called El Floridita, run by bartender Constantino Ribalaigua Vert. El Floridita was a bar famous for its daiquiris, including the twisted versions Vert created, and the story goes that Hemingway ordered a Daiquiri, but without sugar, and with double the amount of rum. At some point the grapefruit juice and maraschino liqueur were added to balance the drink; however, it remains a slightly tart version of a Daiquiri compared with the original – and deliciously so if you ask me.

Ingredients
50ml white rum
20ml lime juice
15ml maraschino liqueur
15ml grapefruit juice

Method
Add all the ingredients to a cocktail shaker. Shake hard over ice and double-strain into a chilled Martini glass or Champagne coupe. Garnish with a lime wedge or wheel.

34		4
	Rc	
	Rude	
	Cosmopolitan	

RUDE COSMOPOLITAN

The Cosmopolitan is a cocktail of many incarnations and many stories. Who invented it is subject to discussion. What is known is that it was New York bartender Dale DeGroff who perfected the recipe when working at Manhattan's Rainbow Rooms in 1996. Dale was the one who added the signature flamed orange zest garnish and helped to popularise the cocktail, which was then featured heavily in HBO series *Sex and the City*, catapulting it into superstardom, with customers calling for it by name in bars all over the world.

The Rude Cosmopolitan uses tequila in place of the vodka (the classic Cosmopolitan often uses citrus-flavoured vodkas). The key is to make sure that your mix of lime juice and tequila is well balanced, and that you don't use too much cranberry juice. That goes for a traditional cosmo too: you're looking for a lightish-pink hue to the cocktail, not a dark-pink or red colour.

Ingredients   30ml tequila (*blanco* or *reposado*)
15ml triple sec
15ml lime juice
30ml cranberry juice

Method   Put all the ingredients into a cocktail shaker. Add ice and shake well before double-straining into a chilled Martini glass. Garnish with a disc of orange zest flambéed over the top of the glass.

To flambé the orange zest, first cut a large(ish) disc of zest from an orange. Make sure there isn't too much pith on the underside of the zest. Hold it between your fingers, peel-side facing the glass. Take a lighter and hold it between the zest and the drink. In one movement squeeze the zest to release the oils, which will sparkle and flame in the lighter's flame. Discard the zest.

SUNDOWNER

A popular drink in South Africa, the sundowners there are made with local brandy and an orange liqueur called Van Der Hum. It's a Martini-style cocktail, but there's a fair amount of juice (both orange and lemon) in proportion to the amount of booze, making it dangerously sippable and the perfect sunset tipple.

A drink very similar to the Sundowner, called the Red Lion, uses gin in place of Cognac, combining orange juice, lemon juice, Grand Marnier and gin (although heavier on the orange liqueur element at 50:50 Grand Marnier to gin); it's also worth a try.

Ingredients   50ml Cognac or brandy
15ml Grand Marnier
15ml orange juice
15ml lemon juice

Method   Add all the ingredients to a cocktail shaker. Shake hard over ice and double-strain into a chilled Martini glass or Champagne coupe. Garnish with a lemon wedge or wheel.

PAINKILLER

The Painkiller is a trademarked cocktail recipe that calls specifically for the inclusion of Pusser's rum. It was created at the Soggy Dollar Bar on the island of Jost Van Dyke in the British Virgin Islands. Why Soggy Dollar? Well, the bar is located on a stretch of beach without a dock, so if you're on a boat nearby and fancy a drink you have to swim to get there, leaving your cash a little wet if you're not careful.

The recipe opposite calls for two parts rum and three parts pineapple juice; however, these ratios are subject to debate, and you'll regularly find recipes calling for two, three or even four parts of the rum. How much you want to add is therefore completely up to you. The ratios opposite are just how I make it. One thing that should be insisted on, though, is fresh pineapple juice, as it really does make a difference in this drink, elevating it to a truly delicious tropical tipple.

Ingredients   50ml Pusser's rum
75ml pineapple juice
25ml orange juice
25ml coconut cream

Method   Add all the ingredients to a cocktail shaker. Shake hard over ice and strain into a highball or hurricane glass. Garnish with grated nutmeg and, in the classic tiki style (see Glossary, page 143), anything else tropical you can lay your hands on: pineapple leaves, orange wedges, maraschino cherries... anything goes.

37   5
Kr
King of
Roses

KING OF ROSES

The King of Roses is a cocktail created by London bartender Will Foster at his bar called Casita, a small yet perfectly formed cocktail bar in Shoreditch, London. A no-nonsense, friendly neighbourhood place, Casita has put an emphasis on fresh ingredients since it opened back in 2005.

The key, therefore, to making the perfect King of Roses is to use freshly squeezed orange juice. The orange juice then combines with the lemon juice, gingerbread syrup (Monin is recommended if you can find it), King's Ginger liqueur and Four Roses bourbon (Four Roses is also a must if you're going to call it a King of Roses), to create a dangerously drinkable thirst-quencher.

Ingredients   50ml Four Roses bourbon
25ml King's Ginger liqueur
10ml gingerbread syrup
25ml lemon juice
50ml orange juice

Method   Add all the ingredients to a cocktail shaker. Add ice and shake well. Double-strain into a chilled Martini glass or Champagne coupe.

38		4
	Bl	
	Blood and Sand	

BLOOD AND SAND

The Blood and Sand is one of a few cocktails that specifically calls for Scotch whisky. Named after a silent black-and-white movie called *Blood and Sand*, directed by Rudolph Valentino, it was created in 1922, the year of the film's release. The first mention of the cocktail in print is in *The Savoy Cocktail Book*, written by Harry Craddock just a few years later in 1930.

With equal amounts of Scotch whisky, sweet vermouth, cherry brandy (the blood) and orange juice (the sand), it does sound a little odd on paper. However, the combination works surprisingly well – although you may want to slightly up the Scotch, and dial back the sweet vermouth or cherry brandy so that it's less sweet. Single-malt whiskies, or a blend of single malts works best, as the spirit needs to stand up to the other ingredients. It's also essential to use a good-quality cherry brandy that's not too sweet, and to use freshly squeezed orange juice if possible.

Ingredients
25ml Scotch whisky
25ml sweet vermouth
25ml cherry brandy
25ml orange juice

Method
Add all the ingredients to a cocktail shaker. Shake over ice and strain into a chilled Martini glass or Champagne coupe*. Garnish with a marachino cherry or a flambéed piece of orange zest (see page 49).

*Some prescribe a double-strain as you've shaken over ice; however, in this instance, I quite like the addition of the small ice shards in the drink that you otherwise catch in the fine strainer.

Fruity and tropical

While there are a few of this style of drinks in the previous group of cocktails, the sixth column is where you'll find the seriously tropical and fruity drinks. They're long, they're juicy, they're fruity and they're a lot of fun! Even the more serious whisky- and bourbon-based drinks get a twist with the addition of raspberries (Bourbon Smash) and pineapple juice (Algonquin).

The thing I love most about the drinks in this column is that they don't take themselves too seriously. They generally don't take too much effort to make, they're easy-drinking at their best, and they're just crying out for over-the-top garnishes – so let your imagination run wild! These are also perfect for summer BBQs.

Column 6

46	4
Bz	
Britz Spritz	

47	3
Ne	
Negroni	

48	3
Mm	
Moscow Mule	

32	4	39	8	49	4
Bk		**Ss**		**B**	
Breakfast Martini		Singapore Sling		Bramble	

33	4	40	6	50	5
Hd		**Hu**		**Mo**	
Hemingway Daiquiri		Hurricane		Mojito	

34	4	41	3	51	4
Rc		**Te**		**Ed**	
Rude Cosmopolitan		Tequila Sunrise		El Diablo	

35	4	42	5	52	7
Su		**Fh**		**Fc**	
Sundowner		Fish House Punch		Fog Cutter	

36	4	43	3	53	5
Pk		**Pp**		**Sc**	
Painkiller		Planter's Punch		Scorpion	

37	5	44	5	54	3
Kr		**Bu**		**Kj**	
King of Roses		Bourbon Smash		Kentucky Mint Julep	

38	4	45	3	55	3
Bl		**Al**		**Wc**	
Blood and Sand		Algonquin		Whisky Cobbler	

SINGAPORE SLING

39 | 8
Ss
Singapore
Sling

The Singapore Sling was created sometime between 1913 and 1915, by Ngiam Tong Boon, a bartender working at the Long Bar in Raffles Hotel in Singapore. That much we know. However, over the years there have been countless recipes for the cocktail listed, and seemingly never two the same. It has even been said that the current version served at the hotel doesn't follow the original recipe, but given half a chance, I'd still go and visit to check it off the cocktail 'to do' list.

Research by cocktail historian David Wondrich has concluded that the original cocktail would have been a gin sling: a mix of gin, citrus (lemon or lime juice), ice, soda water and probably cherry brandy, possibly Benedictine, and maybe bitters. There is no mention of the pineapple juice that is so commonly included nowadays (including in the version now served at Raffles). However, I've played around with the various different recipes, and I do like the cocktail with the addition of the pineapple juice. I've therefore gone with the one on the recipe cards at Raffles. After all, the story did begin there.

Ingredients
30ml gin
7.5ml Cointreau
7.5ml Benedictine
15ml Heering cherry liqueur
15ml lime juice
10ml grenadine
1 dash Angostura bitters
120ml pineapple juice

Method
Add all the ingredients to a cocktail shaker. Add ice, shake, and strain into a highball or sling glass over ice. Serve with a fruit slice (orange or lemon) and a maraschino cherry.

40   6
Hu
Hurricane

HURRICANE

Pat O'Brien's bar in New Orleans officially opened its doors in December 1933; before that you'd need a password to gain entrance as it was Prohibition in the States. It was in this bar that the Hurricane cocktail was invented. The story goes that, during World War II, it was difficult to get hold of Scotch whisky from the UK. Bar owners had to start looking closer to home for their booze, and rum, made in the Caribbean and Latin America was the obvious choice. The bartenders at Pat O'Brien's came up with the Hurricane in 1939 as a way to mix the rum, and served the drink in a hurricane glass – which is shaped and named after the hurricane lamp.

The drink caught on, and they're served in their thousands to this day in the French Quarter of New Orleans, although they're often now served in plastic cups so you can drink them out in the streets (while drinking on the streets is allowed, glass is not).

It's a boozy, rum-laden drink for sure, featuring white and dark rum alongside fruit juices, and when made properly, a tang from the addition of citrus. Many of the classic recipes seem to state lemon juice as the citrus, but for me, lime and rum are perfect bedfellows so I always use lime. Try it for yourself both ways and make up your own mind.

Ingredients
50ml dark rum
50ml light rum
50ml passion fruit juice
25ml orange juice
12ml fresh lime juice
1 bar spoon grenadine

Method
Add all the ingredients except for the grenadine to a cocktail shaker. Add ice, shake, and strain into a hurricane or highball glass over ice. Pour the grenadine into the top of the glass (it is a dense, sticky syrup and will therefore sink to the bottom). Serve with an orange slice and a maraschino cherry.

TEQUILA SUNRISE

Originating in California in the early 1970s, the Tequila Sunrise is one of the drinks I put in the 'disco drinks' category. From Blue Lagoons to June Bugs and Woo Woos, these cocktails are as easy to drink as they are easy to make, and while they're not the most sophisticated cocktails in the world, they're fun. And sometimes that's exactly what you want. In this case, the 'sunrise' is all about the look of the drink when you serve it, the grenadine and orange juice creating a colour gradient from red through orange to yellow in the glass.

Most tequila sunrises will be served in a highball or hurricane glass over ice. An article by drinks expert and cocktail historian David Wondrich suggests serving it in a cocktail/Martini glass, but only if the orange juice is freshly squeezed. I agree that serving it this way looks just as good, if not better, than its longer cousin, but for me, the disco drinks are decidedly summertime drinks – therefore I'd usually go for serving and drinking them over ice so they stay chilled for longer.

Ingredients 50ml tequila
75ml orange juice
1 bar spoon grenadine

Method Add the tequila and orange juice to a cocktail shaker. Fill with ice and shake. Strain into a highball glass filled with ice. Pour the grenadine into the top of the glass; it is a dense, sticky syrup and will therefore sink to the bottom, creating the desired sunshine effect.

FISH HOUSE PUNCH

The Fish House Punch, sometimes known as the Philadelphia Fish House Punch, is one of the most famous punch recipes still relatively well known today. The beauty of punches is that they're perfect for sharing, so don't be afraid to multiply the quantities to make enough for a bowl, as would have been traditional.

The exact origin of this drink is unknown, but there are written references from the late 1700s. It's a balance of ingredients that yields a drink that's not too sweet or too strong. There's also a poem to recite when you serve the Fish House Punch:

There's a little place just out of town,
Where, if you go to lunch,
They'll make you forget your mother-in-law
With a drink called Fish-House Punch.

What was the place out of town? A fishing and social club in Philadelphia called the State in Schuylkill Fishing, where they drank the Fish House Punch as the 'house speciality'.

Ingredients   30ml lemon juice
25ml dark rum
20ml Cognac
10ml peach brandy or crème de peche
10ml sugar syrup (see Glossary, page 143)
25ml water

Method   Add all the ingredients to a cocktail shaker. Add ice and shake, then strain into a highball glass filled with ice.

PLANTER'S PUNCH

The Planter's Punch recipe follows the classic rum-punch proportions of: 1 x sour, 2 x sweet, 3 x strong, and 4 x weak. Created in the late 19th century, there are many different recipes for Planter's Punch; however, the general consensus is that there should be rum, lime and bitters with some sort of sweetening agent, such as sugar syrup or grenadine.

I have included two recipes below, a simple 'classic' style of Planter's Punch, and a more modern incarnation with tropical juices. Both are great drinks, but quite different. The classic is very much like grog, relies on a good-quality rum, and uses water as the 'weak' element – which might sound strange, but results in a tasty cocktail.

The second is longer, fruitier, more tropical and definitely sweeter. For both, I'd recommend adding a few dashes of cocktail bitters such as Angostura to give depth and offset some of the sweetness.

If you're going to make a punch properly, you should really do so in a punchbowl and multiply the quantities below accordingly. After all, punches are designed for parties, groups, friends, and sharing.

'Classic' ingredients

45ml Jamaican rum
15ml lime juice
30ml sugar syrup (see Glossary, page 143)
60ml water

'Modern' ingredients

45ml dark rum
35ml orange juice
35ml pineapple juice
20ml lemon juice
10ml grenadine
10ml sugar syrup (see Glossary, page 143)

Method

Pour all the ingredients into a cocktail shaker. Add ice and shake well. Strain into a highball glass and add cocktail bitters, if desired. Garnish with anything tropical: an orange slice, mint sprig, maraschino cherry, etc.

BOURBON SMASH

One of the first references to the smash cocktail as distinct from the more well-known julep was in *Harry Johnson's Bartenders' Manual* (1882). He included four different smashes in his book: Old Style Whiskey Smash, Fancy Whiskey Smash, Johnson's Fancy Brandy Smash and Medford Rum Smash. They all contain sugar, water, mint, ice and spirit, and then often mention the addition of seasonal fruits.

The difference between smashes and juleps seems a little tenuous, but it appears to be the use of crushed ice in a julep over cubed ice in a smash, and the fact that you don't tend to muddle the mint in the classic julep.

The smash recipe below involves muddling berries (raspberries are preferred, but you can use whatever you can get your hands on) along with the mint.

Ingredients   5–6 berries (raspberries preferred)
6–8 mint leaves
50ml bourbon
25ml lime juice
20ml sugar syrup (see Glossary, page 143)

Method   Gently muddle the raspberries and mint in the bottom of a cocktail shaker. Be careful not to overly muddle the mint, as it will bring out bitter flavours from the leaves. Add the bourbon, lime juice and sugar syrup, along with ice. Shake and strain into an ice-filled highball glass. Garnish with a lime wedge or a mint sprig (or both!). If you use a mint sprig, agitate the leaves by slapping the sprig against your hand to release the mint oils and aromas, then place it next to the straw.

45   3

Al

Algonquin

ALGONQUIN

A rye whiskey Martini of sorts, yet with the unusual addition of pineapple juice, the Algonquin is one of a number of classic cocktails credited to the Algonquin Hotel in New York in the 1930s. The hotel was the site of the infamous Algonquin Round Table, a group of New York's finest minds, who gathered at the hotel, many of them well-known imbibers.

The Algonquin cocktail was unlikely to have been enjoyed by these patrons, as their tastes were famously more boozy – we're talking more straight-up martinis here, rather than drinks that featured juices and other mixers!

You need unsweetened pineapple juice to make a good Algonquin, along with a good-quality vermouth and a spicy rye. The result is a cocktail that's neither too strong nor too weak; it's not too sweet either, and the balance between the spicy rye and the pineapple juice leaves you with a cocktail perfectly suited to pre-dinner tipples.

I'd recommend shaking well to introduce a slight foam on the top of the cocktail, especially if serving on the rocks, as pineapple juice has the benefit of foaming if shaken well. If you want to accentuate the foam, then adding a touch of egg white can help, or use super-fresh pineapple juice. If you don't want foam, then the Algonquin can also be stirred.

Ingredients
45ml rye whiskey
20ml dry vermouth
20ml pineapple juice

Method
Add all the ingredients to a cocktail shaker. Add ice and shake well. Single-strain (so as not to disturb the foam) into a rocks glass over ice, or a Martini glass. Garnish with a large disc of orange zest, squeezing the oils from the peel over the top of the cocktail.

Highballs, swizzled and muddled!

The next chapter and column is a bit of a mishmash. It contains highballs: drinks built over ice and stirred to combine; swizzles: drinks built over crushed ice and 'swizzled' with a stick or a spoon to churn or mix; and muddled drinks: those involving the muddling or crushing of fruit in the bottom of the glass before adding ice and building the rest of the drink.

They're generally not shaken, although you'll find a few in the column that I recommend shaking first, as it gives a better texture and consistency to the drink, and also ensures adequate dilution. This is a group of no-fuss cocktails that are simple to make and delicious to boot.

Column 7

	46 4 **Bz** Britz Spritz	**56** 3 **Az** Aperol Spritz
	47 3 **Ne** Negroni	**57** 3 **A** Americano
	48 3 **Mm** Moscow Mule	**58** 3 **Tw** Twinkle
39 8 **Ss** Singapore Sling	**49** 4 **B** Bramble	**59** 4 **Tc** Tom Collins
40 6 **Hu** Hurricane	**50** 5 **Mo** Mojito	**60** 3 **Cl** Cuba Libre
41 3 **Te** Tequila Sunrise	**51** 4 **Ed** El Diablo	**61** 5 **P** Paloma
42 5 **Fh** Fish House Punch	**52** 7 **Fc** Fog Cutter	**62** 5 **Am** Ambrosia
43 3 **Pp** Planter's Punch	**53** 5 **Sc** Scorpion	**63** 3 **Ds** Dark and Stormy
44 5 **Bu** Bourbon Smash	**54** 3 **Kj** Kentucky Mint Julep	**64** 4 **Ll** Lynchburg Lemonade
45 3 **Al** Algonquin	**55** 3 **Wc** Whisky Cobbler	**65** 6 **Mg** Morning Glory Fizz

BRITZ SPRITZ

The Britz Spritz is a British twist on the Italian-inspired spritz. An evolution of the spritzer, a spritz is distinct from the classic spritzer because of the addition of liqueur, and the use of Prosecco instead of white wine.

The Britz Spritz was invented by Alex Kammerling to showcase his new product: Kamm & Sons, a bittersweet British apéritif created in 2011. The Kamm & Sons takes the place of the liqueur in the spritz, and the classically Italian cocktail is given further British ties by opting for English sparkling wine in place of the Prosecco. Finally British elderflower cordial is also added to sweeten the mixture slightly, a step away from the classic Spritz formula but all the better for it. The result is a delicious summertime drink that is perhaps more accessible to the masses than other spritzes, which are quite bitter due to the use of Italian aperitifs such as Aperol and Campari (see page 82 for an Aperol Spritz recipe).

Ingredients
35ml Kamm & Sons
15ml elderflower cordial
50ml English sparkling wine
50ml soda water

Method
Pour all the ingredients over cubed ice in a glass. Stir well. Squeeze a wedge of grapefruit into the cocktail and garnish with a cucumber slice.

NEGRONI

The Negroni is one of the most well-known Campari cocktails: a liqueur that certainly divides opinion due to its bitter flavour. Personally, I love Campari. However, it's definitely not for everyone – and therefore neither is the Negroni.

Italian Count Camillo Negroni frequented Bar Casoni in Florence in the 1920s. While drinking there he asked the bartender to replace the soda in an Americano with gin, thereby creating a stronger, punchier cocktail, and a cocktail that went on to be named after him: the Negroni.

The Negroni is a simple mix of gin, sweet vermouth and Campari, traditionally in a 1:1:1 ratio. The beauty of the drink is that you can use any well-made gin or sweet vermouth to make it, and while I'm a bit of a stickler on the use of Campari specifically, you can play around by adding other bitter liqueurs like Aperol or Cynar. You can also modify the ratios of the three ingredients: for example, I like my Negronis with slightly more gin (surprise, surprise) than the other ingredients. You may find that certain sweet vermouths are heavier than others, which may also necessitate an amendment to the equal ratios.

The garnish must be orange as far as I'm concerned, but which part of the orange is up to you, and each has its pros and cons. An orange slice or wedge will soak up the mixture, leaving a tasty final act to the drink that I can't help but eat; a piece of orange zest will give a wonderful nose to the drink once the oils are expressed over the top, and a flambéed piece of zest will also add aroma and emphasise the bitterness of the cocktail.

It should also be noted that the Negroni is one of the perfect cocktails for batching. Because it contains no fresh ingredients, it's possible to combine the ingredients in their 1:1:1 ratio in advance. I like to do so and put the pre-measured cocktail into a bottle, storing it in the fridge until needed. I also find that, over time, the ingredients start to mellow, resulting in a beautiful drink.

Ingredients   30ml gin
30ml Campari
30ml sweet vermouth

Method   Add all of the ingredients to an ice-filled rocks glass and stir (usually with a bar spoon, but Negroni enthusiast and cocktail legend gaz regan amusingly prescribes his finger – such is the simplicity of a Negroni!). Garnish with an orange wedge/twist.

MOSCOW MULE

A simple cocktail that began life as a marketing/business idea, and kick-started (pun intended) the American's love affair with vodka, the Moscow Mule is a refreshing cocktail, sure to quench anyone's thirst.

The story goes that friends John G. Martin and Jack Morgan were sat in Jack's pub, the Cock 'n' Bull, in Hollywood in 1946. Back in 1939, John had convinced his boss to shell out quite a bit of cash for a vodka brand called Smirnoff. Things hadn't been going that well since, and sales were not as high as he'd have liked. At the same time, Jack had been bottling ginger beer with the aim of making Americans like it as much as the English did; however, he was finding it equally difficult to shift. An article published in the *New York Herald Tribune* on 28 July 1948 described what happened next under the title 'Experiment with Vodka Lead to Moscow Mule', describing how 'Lime Juice, Ginger Beer and Ice Cubes Are Added to Give Potent New Drink' benefitting all parties involved.

The Moscow Mule is traditionally served in a copper cup, which UK drinks website Difford's Guide attributes to Morgan's girlfriend, who inherited a copper factory that produced the copper mugs. What came next, though, in marketing terms, was simply genius. In 1947, when trying to market the new cocktail, Martin and Morgan commissioned special copper mugs with a kicking mule on the front of them. Martin then acquired one of the recently invented Polaroid cameras and started travelling around the US photographing bartenders holding the cocktail in the copper mug and a bottle of the Smirnoff vodka. One photo remained in the bar (and I can imagine was quite the talking point, given the recent invention).

Simple to make, with a kick from the ginger, a citrus zest from the lime, and a clean booze hit from the vodka, the Moscow Mule is a surprisingly layered drink, considering its limited ingredients. You may also like to throw in a couple of dashes of Angostura; while not traditional, it's a lovely addition.

Ingredients   50ml vodka (Smirnoff if you want to be authentic)
half a lime, juiced
ginger beer

Method   Add the vodka and lime juice to a highball glass or copper cup (you can buy ones with the kicking mule on them online). Fill with ice and top with ginger beer, and optional Angostura bitters, if using.

BRAMBLE

Created in the 1980s by Dick Bradsell at Fred's Club in Soho, London, the Bramble is one of a handful of cocktails now considered to be a modern classic. A cocktail that you can order in any bar in the world, the bartender will not only know it, but will most likely be able to make you one, as it benefits from a simple list of ingredients that combine to make a well-balanced and refreshing drink.

A cross between a cobbler and a sour, the aim was to focus on fresh British ingredients. While many publications list the cocktail as garnished with blackberries in a nod to the inclusion of the crème de mûre (blackberry liqueur), the original featured the much more readily available and commonly stocked raspberry.

The no-fuss name has also aided in its wide uptake, easy to remember (and therefore ask for) in a bar, it is also indicative of the way that the mûre liqueur winds its way through the ice in the glass, as if dodging through brambles.

If you don't have crème de mûre, it is possible to make a variation on the classic Bramble using any berry liqueur. Chambord or crème de framboise work best in my experience.

Ingredients   60ml gin
30ml lemon juice

15ml sugar syrup (see Glossary, page 143)
15ml crème de mûre liqueur

Method   Shake the gin, lemon juice and sugar syrup together in a cocktail shaker. Strain into a rocks glass filled with ice. Stir. Add more crushed ice so that the glass is full. Trickle the crème de mûre over the top and garnish with a lemon wedge and a fresh raspberry.

MOJITO

The origins of the Mojito most likely date back to an old Cuban drink called the Draque, Drake or Drac, supposedly named after Sir Francis Drake from his time in Cuba. A mix of local spirit *aguardiente de cana* (a white, fiery cane spirit, similar to rum), sugar, lime and mint, it was created during the 1500s for its perceived medicinal value.

One author, Ramón de Paula, wrote that he drank '...a little Drake made from *aguardiente de cana* (local cane spirit)' during a cholera epidemic on the island. The vitamin C provided by the lime would have certainly been beneficial, as would the pick-me-up from the aguardiente itself, although as for its ability to ward off or cure cholera... well, we know better now.

At some point in the 1890s the aguardiente was replaced with white rum, and the drink was improved with the addition of ice, which was much more readily available, thanks to efforts by 'Ice King' Frederic Tudor, and then refrigeration pioneer John Gorrie. The Mojito evolved further with the addition of soda water, which I consider to be an optional extra, and one that I don't generally add as I don't think that it's necessary.

When making a Mojito it is important not to crush or grind the mint. The cocktail has enjoyed a massive resurgence in the past decade or so – and rightly so. When made well, it's a clean and refreshing cocktail that is perfect for summer. However, there's one sure-fire way to ruin a Mojito, and that's to over-muddle the mint, as it breaks down the leaves, releasing chlorophyll which has a very bitter and unpleasant taste to it.

So why muddle the mint at all? The reason is simple. The majority of the flavour from mint leaves is olfactory, which means it comes from your sense of smell rather than your taste buds. The next time you eat mint chocolate, hold your nose before the first piece, then release your nose halfway through chewing. It will taste like chocolate alone to begin with, but once you open up your nasal passages you will be able to taste the mint. You can also do this with mint leaves, but trust me: it's nowhere near as much fun! So, muddling the mint in a Mojito is necessary to release the aroma, and therefore the taste, from the leaves of the mint, which is done by lightly muddling or bruising the leaves with the lime juice and sugar syrup. In this vein, the key to a Mojito is to garnish it with a large mint sprig or two, right next to the straw. This means that every sip will be accompanied with the aroma of mint, accentuating the flavour. Be sure to agitate the sprig(s) before placing them in the drink by slapping them against the back of your hand.

Ingredients 20ml lime juice
15ml sugar syrup (see Glossary, page 143)
10–12 mint leaves
50ml white rum
soda water (optional)

Method Add the lime juice, sugar syrup and mint leaves to the bottom of a highball glass. Lightly muddle the mixture. Add the rum and half-fill the glass with crushed ice. Churn with a bar spoon (the round base helps you to pull the mint up through the ice). Fill with more ice and churn again. Top with more ice to fill the glass, finally adding (optional) soda water. The mint sprig garnish should be agitated by slapping it against your hand to release the mint oils and aromas from the leaves, then place it next to the straw.

EL DIABLO

The El Diablo is a simple and refreshing tequila-based cocktail. It consists of lime juice, tequila, crème de cassis and ginger ale. It appears in Trader Vic's publications, sometimes termed the Mexican El Diablo, sometimes simply as El Diablo, which translates as 'The Devil'.
A brilliant summertime thirst-quencher that's easy to prepare, it also scales up well, so you can make a jug on a hot day and share with friends.

Ingredients

50ml tequila
25ml crème de cassis
25ml lime juice
ginger ale

Method

Add the first three ingredients to a highball glass filled with ice. Top with ginger ale and garnish with a lime wedge.

FOG CUTTER

While most tiki cocktails (see Glossary, page 143) tend to sit on the sweet or tropical side, the Fog Cutter, named after a type of diving knife, is drier in flavour – or should be. You therefore need to be careful of the balance, especially in terms of the orgeat syrup used, and you should use freshly squeezed orange juice wherever possible. As with most tiki cocktails, recipes for the Fog Cutter appear in both Beachbum Berry's and Trader Vic's cocktail publications.

In *Trader Vic's Bartender's Guide* (1947), he remarks, 'After two of these, you won't even see the stuff.' Don't let its colour, from the orange juice, deceive you: this cocktail packs quite the punch!

It's important to drink cocktails with alcohol 'floating' on the top with a straw; otherwise the first sip you take will consist entirely of the floated product (in this case, Sherry). Some recipes (including the one by Trader Vic) involve floating cherry brandy rather than Sherry. Worth a try, but I'm a sucker for Sherry so I stick with the Beachbum formula.

Ingredients   40ml lemon juice
20ml orange juice
10ml orgeat syrup
40ml white rum
20ml brandy
10ml gin
10ml sweet or cream Sherry

Method   Pour all the ingredients except the sherry into a cocktail shaker. Shake hard with ice. Strain into a highball glass filled with ice. Slowly pour the Sherry into the glass to float it over the other ingredients (some prefer to 'cap' the cocktail with crushed ice before adding the Sherry to help it to sit on the top of the drink). Garnish with mint.

SCORPION

The Scorpion is also known as the Scorpion Bowl, as it was typically served as a punch for several people. It's often stated that the punch should be garnished with gardenia flowers, which float on the top. Typically, a Scorpion punch would be drunk straight from the bowl with long straws.

The recipe below makes a single cocktail. However, if you want to make it into a punch, just multiply the quantities. The single serve can be shaken or blended with crushed ice; the latter is especially tasty on a hot summer's day. When making it as a punch, it's likely that the mixture will sit around for a while, and because you don't want to end up with an overdiluted mixture, I recommend building the punch as per the method below.

Ingredients   50ml white rum
20ml brandy or Cognac
50ml orange juice
30ml lemon juice
20ml orgeat syrup

Method   Shaken: Add all the ingredients to a cocktail shaker. Add ice and shake well before straining into an ice-filled highball glass. Garnish with an edible flower or a sprig of mint.

Blended: Add all the ingredients to a cocktail shaker along with a highball glass full of crushed ice. Shake well and serve in a highball glass. Garnish with an edible flower or a sprig of mint.

Punch serve: Add all the ingredients to a punchbowl (the more kitsch, the better), add a single large ice cube if possible (freeze water overnight in a food container). Once you've built the punch, stir thoroughly and leave for around 30 minutes to an hour to chill adequately and dilute. Before serving, stir again – this is where a ladle can be doubly useful – and garnish with edible flowers if you can get hold of them.

KENTUCKY MINT JULEP

The 'official' cocktail of Derby Day in Kentucky, the Mint Julep has become an iconic drink due to the sheer number of them served on the day (some estimates put it at over 100,000 each year), and the traditional silver or pewter cups they are made in. It is a refreshing drink for a hot day, due to the use of mint and crushed ice, but be under no illusions: a julep is a strong drink that packs a punch – it's basically bourbon over crushed ice with a couple of added extras. The reason it's served over crushed ice is not only to chill the drink, but also because the cocktail should slowly dilute as you're drinking it.

The Churchill Downs clubhouse, home of the Kentucky Derby, had been making juleps for a number of years. It was a simple choice of cocktail to offer due to an abundance of mint growing nearby and the local bourbon spirit available quite literally by the barrel-load. However, when the cocktail was given a makeover in 1939, which is also when the management decided to serve the juleps in commemorative cups, the julep became both easily recognised and unique in the serve, starting it on the road to becoming the iconic classic cocktail it's considered to be today.

The julep cup (or glass tumbler, if you don't have access to one) should be well chilled prior to use, which is best done by placing it in the freezer for a few hours. This prevents the crushed or cracked ice from melting too quickly. To crush the ice, wrap it in a clean, thick towel (or get your hands on a Lewis Ice Bag with reinforced stitched sides) and hammer with a muddler, rolling pin or joiner's mallet until you have small chunks. Others prefer to crack the ice, as they believe the drink benefits from slightly larger chunks of ice. To do this put a cube of ice in the palm of your hand and tap firmly with the back of a spoon. This can be a little tricky and more time-consuming to achieve, so if I'm making a batch I tend to go with crushed by way of hammering the ice in a Lewis bag. Just be careful not to overly crush; otherwise you end up with 'snow' that will melt far too quickly, overdiluting your drink.

There are many variations of the julep, which include the use of just about every other spirit, from rye whiskey, to gin, brandy, Calvados, whisky, Cognac and even rum. However, the true Kentucky Mint Julep should only be made with bourbon.

A simple mix of just three ingredients, the key is to balance the sweetness from the sugar syrup with the inherent sweetness of the bourbon. Do not oversweeten the mixture. The beauty of building the drink is that you can add more of any ingredient as you're making it, tasting as you go, so I'd always be cautious about the amount of sugar syrup you add at first. You can always add more, but trying to pull the balance back from an overly sweetened julep is much more difficult.

Ingredients   10–12 mint leaves
60ml bourbon
20ml sugar syrup (see Glossary, page 143)

Method   Add all of the ingredients to your chilled julep cup or rocks glass. Stir gently. If possible leave for 10 minutes or so for the mint to infuse. Others infuse mint into a bottle of bourbon overnight, which is great for parties, but just be sure not to leave the mint for too long, as unpleasant and bitter flavours will start to appear. Add crushed ice and churn with a spoon (preferably a bar spoon – the metal disc on one end makes pulling the mint up through the ice super-easy). Top up with more ice and churn again. Finally, cap with ice (in a small mound on top, if you can, for aesthetic reasons), and garnish with a mint sprig or two. You should agitate the mint sprig by slapping it against the back of the hand before placing it into the drink alongside your straws. The key is to make sure every sip is met with a noseful of mint aroma, enhancing the flavour of the cocktail.

WHISKY COBBLER

Cobblers are an old family of cocktails that consist of spirit, sugar and fresh fruit. You can use any spirit (or wine for that matter; they began with Sherry) to make a cobbler. Like the julep, the cobbler family is without doubt an American creation, and came about at a time when ice and straws were something of a novelty, being new innovations of the time.

Jerry Thomas dedicates a chapter to the cobbler in his *Bartenders Guide or How To Mix Drinks: The Bon Vivant's Companion* (1862), describing seven different types using Sherry, Champagne, catawba wine, hock, claret, Sauternes and (unique as it's the only spirit-based cobbler) whisky. They are all quite similar in their make-up, the difference being that he prescribed orange slices in the Whisky Cobbler.

Thomas fully admits that cobblers are simple to make, but the key is that he states that 'in order to make it acceptable to the eye as well as the palate, it is necessary to display some taste in ornamenting the glass'. This has come to mean the use of fruit (especially seasonal berries) and herbs (particularly mint) to garnish the drink once done. The key, however, is that this is for ornamental reasons only, and should never be shaken along with the whisky and sugar.

Traditionally, cobblers would have used icing sugar, but I tend to use sugar syrup for ease. It's much easier to control the amount of sweetness you add, means you don't have to shake it for as long and there's also no chance of grains of sugar finding their way into the drink, causing a crunchy finish.

I really like the Thomas recipe that includes the orange slices with the whisky and sugar, yet there are various other recipes for a Whisky Cobbler, especially those created recently, that substitute an orange liqueur for the sugar, and those that prescribe lemon over orange. So long as you follow the formula of lots of whisky along with some sugar/syrup and citrus, you're going to end up with a tasty drink. The key is always to serve over crushed ice; as with a julep, there's a lot of booze and not much else in a cobbler, so you need to take advantage of the ice to aid dilution.

Ingredients   50ml Scotch whisky
1 teaspoon sugar (or 20ml sugar syrup; see Glossary, page 143)
2–3 orange slices

Method   Put all the ingredients into a cocktail shaker. Add ice and shake well. Strain into a wine glass or julep cup filled with crushed ice. Garnish with a mint sprig and seasonal berries – or whatever else you'd like to throw on top!

Collinses, spritzes and fizz

A group of cocktails that all employ carbonation, the Collins, spritzes and fizz are ideal for those who love fizzy drinks. Whether it be soda water, Champagne, Prosecco, ginger ale, cola or lemonade, these cocktails combine fizz with spirit to great effect.

The Collins cocktail family even has a glass named after it, which is generally thinner and taller than a traditional highball. They consist of spirit, sweetening agent, citrus and soda. The fizz family is basically the same as the Collins family, although they're generally served in smaller glasses and can also contain egg white, as with the Ramos Gin Fizz.

A spritz is a wine-based cocktail popular in northeast Italy, consisting of Prosecco, a bitter liqueur and sparkling water. An evolution of the spritzer (wine and soda), a spritz is distinct due to the addition of a liqueur and the use of Prosecco. A perfect pre-dinner apéritif, the spritz category has seen a revival over the past few years in the UK, driven by Aperol, which has specifically championed the Aperol Spritz.

Column 8

46 4 **Bz** Britz Spritz	56 3 **Az** Aperol Spritz	
47 3 **Ne** Negroni	57 3 **A** Americano	
48 3 **Mm** Moscow Mule	58 3 **Tw** Twinkle	66 7 **Bm** Bloody Mary
49 4 **B** Bramble	59 4 **Tc** Tom Collins	67 7 **Rs** Red Snapper
50 5 **Mo** Mojito	60 3 **Cl** Cuba Libre	68 7 **Cu** Cubanita
51 4 **Ed** El Diablo	61 5 **P** Paloma	69 11 **Ba** Bandera
52 7 **Fc** Fog Cutter	62 5 **Am** Ambrosia	70 7 **Po** Prairie Oyster
53 5 **Sc** Scorpion	63 3 **Ds** Dark and Stormy	
54 3 **Kj** Kentucky Mint Julep	64 4 **Ll** Lynchburg Lemonade	71 8 **Bd** Bloody Derby
55 3 **Wc** Whisky Cobbler	65 6 **Mg** Morning Glory Fizz	72 7 **Bj** Bloody Joseph

APEROL SPRITZ

Aperol is often touted as Campari's less bitter and more accessible sister, which definitely rings true. The Aperol Spritz is therefore a bittersweet cocktail, especially when paired with a good-quality Prosecco (there's no need to spend huge amounts of money here, but you are going to want a decent-quality fizz).

The recipe below makes a decent-sized cocktail, but if you want to make a jug for a picnic, just remember the ratio of 3:2:1 (Prosecco:spirit:soda). You can also substitute the Aperol for all other manner of apéritifs, bitters and liqueurs. I'm a massive fan of using St-Germain elderflower liqueur, as is my mum!

Ingredients   75ml Prosecco
50ml Aperol
25ml soda water

Method   Add all the ingredients to a glass filled with ice. Stir and garnish with an orange wedge or slice.

AMERICANO

The Americano cocktail (not to be confused with the Americano coffee) is the precursor to the Negroni (see page 66).

The Americano is thought to be an evolution of another cocktail, the Milano-Torino. This simple mix of Campari (from Milan) and Martini Rosso Vermouth (from Turin) was served on the rocks with an orange twist. The addition of soda water transforms the Milano-Torino into the Americano and the longer apéritif drink we are familiar with today.

Ingredients   50ml Campari
50ml sweet vermouth (Martini Rosso preferably)
soda water

Method   Fill a highball glass with ice. Add the Campari and sweet vermouth. Top with soda water, stir to mix, and garnish with a wedge of orange.

TWINKLE

The Twinkle is a simple refreshing Champagne cocktail created in 2002 by Tony Conigliaro while he was working at The Lonsdale in London. It is a ludicrously simple cocktail to make – that's the beauty of it – however, it's a cocktail that you can easily twist to your own tastes too.

To adapt the Twinkle for your own, start by substituting the elderflower liqueur or cordial for other flavours. By looking to seasonal ingredients you can create drinks specifically for summer (strawberry), autumn (rhubarb), or take inspiration from the time of year in other ways (ginger for Christmas cocktails, perhaps?). You may find you need to play around with the proportion of vodka to liqueur depending on the sweetness of the liqueur you use, and you may also find that sometimes the addition of 10ml or so of citrus can be beneficial. The Twinkle, however, is just perfect the way it is.

Ingredients   25ml vodka
15ml elderflower liqueur or cordial
Champagne (around 75ml)

Method   Add the vodka and elderflower liqueur to a cocktail shaker. Shake well and double-strain into a chilled Champagne flute or coupe. Top with Champagne. Garnish with a long twist of lemon zest.

TOM COLLINS

The Tom Collins is a simple, classic gin cocktail consisting of gin, lemon juice, sugar syrup and soda water. Think of as a boozy traditional lemonade.

The first recipe for the Tom Collins appears in the second edition of *Jerry Thomas' Bartenders Guide or How To Mix Drinks: The Bon Vivant's Companion*, published in 1876. The Collins is a style of drink where the 'Tom' element changes, depending on what spirit you use. For example, the John Collins contains bourbon.

The original Tom Collins, though, is likely to have come about through what is potentially the worst prank in the history of jokes. OK, OK: maybe not *that* bad, but it's definitely up there. The story goes that in New York, people would ask a friend or colleague if they'd seen Tom Collins, because they'd overheard him talking harshly about them. The idea was to get a rise out of the friend to make them look like a bit of an idiot. The joke was, of course, that there was no Tom Collins. As I said, hilarious, right? The friend was usually encouraged to seek out Tom Collins at a nearby local bar, so making him or her look like a fool in front of a number of people when the barkeep was asked where to find the elusive man. The timing of the hoax (1874) and when the first recipe appeared (1876) makes it more than likely that some clever bartender came up with the cocktail because of the hoax to make a few quid out of it.

The Gettysburg Compiler, a newspaper published in Gettysburg, Pennsylvania, was just one of the newspapers that reported the hoax. The following excerpt is taken from 1874:

'Have you seen Tom Collins?
If you haven't, perhaps you had better do so, and as quick as you can, for he is talking about you in a very rough manner – calling you hard names, and altogether saying things about you that are rather calculated to induce people to believe there is nothing you wouldn't steal short of a red-hot stove. Other little things of that nature he is openly speaking in public places, and as a friend – although of course we don't wish to make you feel uncomfortable – we think you ought to take some notice of them and of Mr. Tom Collins.'

This is about the cheerful substance of a very successful practical joke which has been going the rounds of the city in the past week. It is not to this manor born, but belongs to New York, where it was played with immense success to crowded houses until it played out.

The beauty of the Tom Collins is that you can not only mix things up by changing the base spirit (vodka, bourbon, whisky and tequila all work well), but you can also use different sweetening agents in place of the sugar syrup when you use flavoured liqueurs such as St-Germain (elderflower), crème de framboise (raspberry) or maraschino liqueur (cherry).

Ingredients   50ml gin
25ml lemon juice
20ml sugar syrup (see Glossary, page 143)
soda water

Method   Fill a highball glass with ice. Add the gin, lemon juice and sugar syrup. Top with soda, add more ice if necessary to fill the glass, and stir to mix. Garnish with a lemon wedge, a maraschino cherry or, if you've twisted it up using a different liqueur, anything appropriate.

CUBA LIBRE

The Cuba Libre, meaning 'Free Cuba', came out of Cuba's War of Independence in the 1890s. As with much cocktail history, who exactly named the drink is up for debate, but during the American intervention in Cuba, the term 'Cuba Libre' was used a great deal by Cubans and Americans in the country.

The simple yet refreshing mix of rum, cola and lime isn't exactly the most innovative cocktail, and recently it has become part of a family of cocktails (like the Screwdriver) where an order of one will instantly make the bartender wonder if you're just a know-it-all, since it is just a rum and Coke with fresh lime. However, make sure you get the ratio of lime to rum to cola just right (don't over-dilute with the cola, and don't over-citrus with the lime) and there's no arguing that it's anything but a potent, tasty drink.

Given its simplicity, I never measure out lime juice when making a Cuba Libre; 2–3 wedges should do, depending on how juicy they are. I also very rarely measure the rum at home, but for weights, measures, responsible drinking, etc., I've included it below. I also sometimes like to add a couple of drops of Angostura bitters. Definitely not classic, but tasty nonetheless.

Ingredients
2–3 lime wedges
50ml rum
70–100ml Coca-Cola

Method
Fill a highball glass with ice. Squeeze in the lime wedges, add the rum, and finally add the cola. Add more ice to fill the glass (the more, the better to slow dilution), or more cola if needed, but be careful not to overdilute the rum.

61	5
P	
Paloma	

PALOMA

Salt and tequila are famous bedfellows, even if (in my opinion), shooting a good-quality tequila after filling your mouth with salt, before then chasing the taste away with lime juice is a total waste. Salt and grapefruit, however, are a great mix for good reason: salt can help to soften the acidity from citrus without needing to add excess sweetening agents. Add a pinch of salt to a citrussy drink and it's surprisingly refreshing on hot summer days and can help to replace electrolytes lost due to sweat. Just ask any fans of the Greyhound cocktail!

Why all this talk of salt? Well, the Paloma cocktail famously comes in a glass with salt on the rim, with the cocktail containing grapefruit, lime, tequila and agave syrup. These ingredients combine to produce a cocktail that's sweet, sour, bitter and salty, getting all of your taste buds working in your mouth. Made well, it's a hell of a drink.

Some do away with the salt rim, especially recently when salt has gotten a bit of a bad rep in the press for health reasons (you actually need a little salt in your diet; it's vast amounts that are the problem). So, unless you're then going to add a pinch of salt to the cocktail itself (perfectly OK by me), I wouldn't lose it. The drink just isn't the same.

Grapefruit soda used to be pretty tricky to get hold of in the UK, but you'll now find a brand called Ting stocked in large supermarkets, usually with the ginger beer in the world-food aisles. I'd definitely recommend stocking up on it once you find it; it's a fantastically versatile mixer that goes well with most spirits, including gin, rum, tequila (obviously) and vodka.

Ingredients
60ml tequila
20ml lime juice
10ml agave syrup
60ml pink grapefruit juice
grapefruit soda

Method
Rub a lime wedge around the edge of a highball glass. Put a tablespoon or so of salt on to a plate, then, holding the glass at a 90 degree angle to the plate, coat the rim of the glass with the salt (the lime juice will help it to stick). Fill the glass with ice. In the meantime, add the tequila, lime juice, agave syrup and pink grapefruit juice to a cocktail shaker. Add ice, shake, and strain into the salt-rimmed glass. Top with grapefruit soda.

62   5
Am
Ambrosia

AMBROSIA

In 1918, Count Arnaud Cazenave opened the now-infamous Arnaud's restaurant in New Orleans. A huge advocate of good food and great cocktails, he unfortunately opened just before Prohibition hit the States. Like all great heroes, Arnaud defied the authorities, and continued to serve liquor in coffee cups. He was caught and imprisoned, but was able to charm his way out of the charges, thus cementing his legendary status.

Arnaud's restaurant is responsible for creating many interesting cocktails, including the house signature, Arnaud's Special Cocktail: a pretty potent mix of Scotch, Dubonet Rouge and orange bitters. The Ambrosia was one such cocktail, and perhaps a little more accessible than the 'Special'. It is definitely the one that Count Arnaud and his restaurant tend to be known for.

Reference to the Ambrosia in *The Encyclopedia of American Food and Drink* by John F. Mariani (1983) states that the cocktail was first concocted just after the end of Prohibition in the 1920s – but given the reputation of Count Arnaud, who's really going to believe that?

One of the lesser-known classics, the Ambrosia is still well worth a try. It's a lovely Champagne cocktail that's sure to impress – so long as your guests aren't expecting something custardy, due to the UK custard brand of the same name! Plus, you can wow them with your Greek mythology knowledge as the cocktail is named after ambrosia, the food and drink of the gods. It was said that any mortal who ate or drank ambrosia became immortal. After a couple of these, you may just think that's possible.

Ingredients
25ml Cognac
25ml Calvados
5ml triple sec
5ml lemon juice
Champagne

Method
Pour all the ingredients except for the Champagne into a cocktail shaker. Add ice and shake well. Strain into a chilled Champagne flute or Champagne coupe, top up with Champagne and serve immediately.

DARK AND STORMY

The national drink of Bermuda, a Dark and Stormy (or Dark 'n' Stormy) must be made with Gosling's Black Seal Rum – at least that's what they'll tell you if you ask. That said, the Bermudans don't include lime in their recipes, which, for me, is a must. So, if you don't have any Gosling's to hand and use a different rum... well, I won't tell if you don't. Just make sure it's a good-quality, big-tasting dark rum!

As for the ginger beer, there's a brand from Bermuda called Barritts if you're going for authenticity. Gosling's has recently brought out its own brand especially for a Dark and Stormy, which does very nicely too.

The history of the Dark and Stormy, unsurprisingly for a rum drink, harks back to sailors in the navy. In the 1800s, rum rations for the British Royal Navy (yes, that was A Thing – all the way up until 1970) were sourced from the Caribbean Islands on which the officers were based. Sailors received an eighth of a pint a day, equivalent to two ounces or 60ml of rum. Ginger beer was a British creation, and for whatever reason (perhaps as ginger is known to calm sea sickness), made its way across the Atlantic and started to be mixed with the rations of rum. The rest, as they say, is history.

The Dark and Stormy is arguably a twist on a mule, the only difference being the specific type of rum called for. When making the cocktail, you can therefore build the cocktail as you would a mule (listed as the Simple method on page 90), or add the ginger beer and lime before floating the dark rum on top (listed as the D&S method). The dark rum 'floating' on top of the ginger beer gives the illusion of dark storm clouds – appropriate given the name!

The beauty of the cocktail is that it's fairly difficult to mess up. Yes, you could add a bit too much lime or ginger beer, but just put in a bit more rum to compensate, and you'll soon balance it back out. This makes it a brilliant drink to make in batches or in a jug or punchbowl to share with friends.

Ingredients
50ml dark rum
15ml lime juice
150ml ginger beer

Method
Simple: Fill a highball glass with ice. Pour in the rum and lime juice, top with ginger beer.
D&S: Fill a highball glass with ice. Pour in the ginger beer, leaving a window for the lime and rum. Squeeze in the lime then slowly pour over the dark rum to float it on top.

LYNCHBURG LEMONADE

Named after Lynchburg, Tennessee, the home of Jack Daniel's, the Lynchburg Lemonade is like a grown-up's traditional lemonade. Very similar to the gin-based Tom Collins (page 83), the sugar syrup is replaced with orange-flavoured triple sec to complement the whiskey, which takes the place of the gin.

Ingredients
40ml Jack Daniel's whiskey
20ml triple sec
25ml lemon juice
lemonade

Method
Add the whiskey, triple sec and lemon juice to a cocktail shaker. Add ice and shake well. Strain into a highball glass filled with ice and top with lemonade. Stir gently and garnish with a lemon wheel or wedge.

MORNING GLORY FIZZ

Putting all jokes aside, the Morning Glory Fizz is a cocktail perfectly suited for drinking in the morning or early afternoon. A reviving mixture of Scotch whisky, citrus, sugar syrup, egg white, absinthe and soda water, it's sure to perk up just about anyone in the morning!

First seen in *Harry Johnson's Bartenders' Manual* (1882), the cocktail can also be found in Hugo R. Ensslin's *Recipes for Mixed Drinks* (1916), and *The Savoy Cocktail Book* by Harry Craddock (1930). Each recipe is slightly different, with the differences mostly centring around the type of citrus to use: lemon, lime, or both. I tend to sit more on the side of using both, as the blend of the two is the best of both worlds when paired against the Scotch and sugar.

As for the Scotch, a good blend is all you need, so don't shell out on the expensive single malts. Make the most of the multitude of styles of whisky and try different types; blends that incorporate heavier peated whiskies can work particularly well.

The Morning Glory Fizz is very similar in many ways to the Ramos Gin Fizz. Both contain spirit, citrus and egg white, and are then topped up with soda. If you've ever heard about the Ramos, well, it's not the easiest of cocktails to make, as it requires an extremely long shake. The benefit of this cocktail over the Ramos, however, is that it doesn't contain cream – and the cream is part of the reason why such a long shake is required. That's not to say that this isn't a cocktail where it's really important to shake thoroughly, though; the key is to make sure that the drink has been shaken sufficiently so that the texture is silky-smooth. But you're not going to need a line of 'shaker boys' as they did to make Ramoses in the late 1800s in New Orleans!

Ingredients
50ml Scotch whisky
25ml lemon/lime juice mix (50:50)
15ml sugar syrup (see Glossary, page 143)
egg white
1–2 dashes absinthe
soda water

Method
Add all the ingredients except the soda water to a cocktail shaker. Shake without ice to emulsify the egg white. Add ice and shake again. Strain into a highball glass (no ice), and top up to the top with soda water.

Snappers

Column 9

56 3 **Az** Aperol Spritz		
57 3 **A** Americano		
58 3 **Tw** Twinkle	**66** 7 **Bm** Bloody Mary	**73** 3 **Wr** White Russian
59 4 **Tc** Tom Collins	**67** 7 **Rs** Red Snapper	**74** 3 **Ax** Alexander
60 3 **Cl** Cuba Libre	**68** 7 **Cu** Cubanita	**75** 3 **Pc** Piña Colada
61 5 **P** Paloma	**69** 11 **Ba** Bandera	**76** 5 **Df** Death Flip
62 5 **Am** Ambrosia	**70** 7 **Po** Prairie Oyster	**77** 6 **Eg** Eggnog
63 3 **Ds** Dark and Stormy		**78** 3 **Ru** Rum Flip
64 4 **Ll** Lynchburg Lemonade	**71** 8 **Bd** Bloody Derby	**79** 4 **Bo** Boston Flip
65 6 **Mg** Morning Glory Fizz	**72** 7 **Bj** Bloody Joseph	**80** 4 **Ic** Irish Coffee

This column of the main table is concerned with Bloody Marys, Red Snappers and all types of tomato-based libations.

The most well-known cocktail of the lot is the Bloody Mary; however I have taken a leaf from gaz regan's (the bartender formerly known as Gary Regan's) knowledgeable book and have termed the category or family 'snappers'. Some of the cocktails in this snapper family follow the formula you'll recognise from the vodka-based Bloody Mary or the gin-based Red Snapper; others are a little further afield. To reduce repetition as far as the recipe pages go, I'll start with a basic formula for a snapper (tomato plus spirit plus herbs, spices and sauces) before introducing each variant specifically.

The classic snapper cocktails like the Bloody Mary and the Red Snapper are both basic and complex. You can walk into any pub or bar and get a vodka and tomato juice, and many of them will then hand you some Tabasco and Worcestershire sauce to add to your own preference, creating what is essentially a Bloody Mary. However, there are also a million and one possibilities and ingredients you can add to make a 'proper' Bloody Mary. Plus, a lot of what you add, and the quantity you choose to include, will be due to individual taste – more so than with most other cocktails, due to people's wildly varying capacities to tolerate spice.

The basic formula for a snapper

Ingredients
50ml spirit
100ml tomato juice
Tabasco sauce (4–10 drops, depending on your preferred level of spice)
Worcestershire sauce (2–5 drops, depending on your preferred level of umami: i.e. how savoury you would like your cocktail)
lemon juice (a few ml)
black pepper (1–2 twists of a pepper grinder)
salt (celery salt if preferred; only use a pinch)

Method   Add all the ingredients to a cocktail shaker, adding the
Tabasco and Worcestershire sauces to taste, and the
quantity of lemon juice depending on preference. Add
ice and roll the cocktail shaker, turning it over and over
slowly to allow the ingredients to mix and the drink to
chill. Be careful not to over-agitate or dilute the mixture.
Strain into a chilled highball glass, with or without ice
(depending on your preference).

Garnish

Unusually for cocktails in this book, the garnish for a
snapper gets its own section. The now-synonymous
celery stick used to garnish a Bloody Mary is said to
have originated in the 1960s in a hotel in Chicago, when
a guest had the stroke of genius to stir this savoury
cocktail with a celery crudité.

These days, pretty much anything goes. I've seen
snappers garnished with carrot sticks, rosemary sprigs
and basil leaves, with simple additions, such as a lemon
wedge or cherry tomato, to something as elaborate as
a bacon sandwich served on the side (no, really!). I've
even seen Red Snappers (containing gin) garnished with
juniper berries and other botanicals from the gin.

I tend to be a fan of keeping things simple, so a
celery stick works perfectly well for me, with the added
bonus that you can use it as a stirring stick if you don't
eat it too quickly (but then again, I'm also a sucker for a
bacon sandwich...).

Some places also like to add a salt rim to the glass,
although if you're going to do this, I wouldn't put the
salt into the cocktail too; you don't want to over-salt it.
Salt and tomato juice combine to amplify the umami,
savoury taste of the snapper. Celery salt is used
frequently, as is the practice of mixing a few dried chilli
flakes into the salt.

One of the biggest surprises I ever encountered
when judging a cocktail competition was a mystery
box round, where the bartenders, when presented with

popping candy, mixed it with celery salt and freshly ground black pepper and used it to rim a glass for a snapper variation. Every pop from the candy came with a burst of celery, salt and fresh pepper flavour. It was unexpectedly brilliant!

Tomato juice

The key to a good snapper is to use fresh, good-quality tomato juice. If there's one thing to spend a bit of extra cash on, it's not the booze; it's not the fancy and unusual seasonings (see a list of ingredients sometimes used in snappers below): it's the tomato juice. Stay away from long-life versions that tend to be filled with sugar and miss the zing you get from fresh juice. Some prescribe the use of passata in snappers, but these can be overly thick and make the cocktail more like a gazpacho soup than a cocktail.

Fresh tomato juice has the added benefit of having a thicker mouthfeel and texture that is so important in a snapper without having to go down the passata route. Tomato juice is a little bit of a tricky beast, in that it's a thixotropic fluid. This means that it becomes thinner when agitated (e.g. through stirring or shaking), and is thicker when it has been left to stand. This also means that no matter how much time and money you spend on a fresh tomato juice with a thick, unctuous mouthfeel, you're going to need to treat it carefully if you want to preserve its properties in your snapper. That's why rolling is the prescribed method of making any cocktail containing tomato juice, where you gently roll the cocktail shaker over and over (or up and down) to achieve dilution and chill the drink without agitating the juice too much.

Other commonly (and some not so commonly) used ingredients in snappers

horseradish
wasabi
Sherry

sugar (to counter the lemon juice and accentuate the
   tomato flavour)
balsamic vinegar
soy sauce
cayenne pepper
herbs: rosemary, basil, thyme
smoked paprika
olives, or olive brine
capers, or caper brine
clamato juice (yep, that's tomato juice and clam broth –
   you can thank the Canadians for that!)
beef consommé or bouillon

BLOODY MARY

The Bloody Mary is the original snapper, said to have
been created in the 1920s by a French bartender working
in Harry's New York Bar in Paris. Fernand Petiot came up
with a 50:50 mix of vodka and tomato juice, both of which
were fairly new introductions to the drinking classes at
the time. Fast-forward nearly 100 years and Bloody Marys
today contain a greater proportion of tomato juice to
vodka than Petiot's version, include spices and sauces,
and are traditionally garnished with a stick of celery.
Follow the basic snapper formula using vodka as your
spirit. A dry Sherry makes a particularly great addition to
a Bloody Mary, usually floated on top of the drink.

RED SNAPPER

The Red Snapper is gin-based. Also created by Fernand
Petiot upon his move to New York in the 1940s. The
beauty of using gin rather than vodka is that, due to the
botanical make-up of gins, there tends to be a greater
variety in terms of flavour than among vodkas. You can
therefore use a citrus-flavoured gin to make a lighter and
fresher snapper, a cardamom-heavy gin to accentuate
the spice, or a more herbal-flavoured gin paired with an
interesting garnish such as rosemary or thyme.

CUBANITA

The Cubanita is a rum-based snapper best made with white rum. Take inspiration from the rum-producing areas of the world, traditionally the Caribbean and Latin America, in your herbs and spices for your Cubanita. I once tried a Cubanita that included jerk seasoning and it was utterly delicious!

BANDERA

The Bandera, or perhaps better-named the *Tequila con Verdita con Sangrita* is a little unusual for cocktails included in this book as it's technically a series of shots rather than a cocktail. However, the process behind making the shots that sit on either side of the tequila could be considered cocktails in themselves (virgin cocktails, but cocktails nevertheless), and therefore it seemed apt, and a bit of fun, to include them.

Bandera stands for flag, and this series of shots features a green shot, a clear shot and a red shot, reflecting the colours of the Mexican flag. It's a traditional way to drink tequila – none of that salt nonsense – and while it can be taken as three consecutive shots, it is traditionally drunk by sipping each shot over time, usually accompanied by a beer.

The middle shot is tequila – that much is simple. But make sure you use a decent variety; look for something that has been made from 100 per cent agave.

The green shot taken first is often just lime juice, however, the recipe below is for something a little more fun called *verdita*. The verdita recipe I've included is the one that has put one little London bar, Casita, on the map. The bar has become somewhat of a destination for its verdita, which was first made at the sadly closed Green and Red tequila bar down the road. In Casita, it is served to be drunk after the tequila (they don't serve sangrita) and the combination is more than worth a trip to try.

The sangrita recipe included below is the one that I make at home. It includes tomato juice and pomegranate juice. There is some debate about whether sangrita should contain tomato juice, depending on where in Mexico you are, and whose sangrita you're drinking, as each bar (and often family) has its own secret recipe. However, I prefer to include the tomato, to give the juicy, umami flavour against the sweetness of the pomegranate juice.

Verdita ingredients

(makes around 1 litre)
1 bunch coriander
1 bunch mint
1–2 fresh jalapeño pepper (depending on how hot you like it)
1 carton pineapple juice
Note: bunches of coriander are usually larger than mint; this recipe takes this into account.

Method

Add all the ingredients to a blender. Blend thoroughly. Strain through a sieve and store the resulting liquid in a bottle until needed (last 2–3 days but best when fresh).

Sangrita ingredients

(makes just over 500ml)
200ml tomato juice
200ml pomegranate juice
100ml lime juice
50ml hot pepper sauce
1 teaspoon salt
1 teaspoon freshly ground black pepper

Method

Add all the ingredients to a cocktail shaker. Add ice and roll the cocktail shaker, turning it over and over slowly to allow the ingredients to mix and the drink to chill. Strain into a bottle until needed (last 2–3 days but best when fresh).

PRAIRIE OYSTER

The infamous Prairie Oyster doesn't actually contain tomato juice, but it contains so many of the other ingredients now synonymous with a snapper that it seemed to fit well here in the table.

A 19th century hangover cure, the traditional recipe didn't specify alcohol; however, modern recipes seem to prescribe a glug of Cognac – and who's to argue with adding a little extra 'hair of the dog' to a hangover cure?

Ingredients   15ml Cognac
5ml vinegar (red wine/white wine/cider – it's up to you)
4–5 dashes Worcestershire sauce
3–5 dashes Tabasco
pinch salt
pinch freshly ground black pepper
1 egg yolk

Method   Add the Cognac, vinegar, Worcestershire sauce, Tabasco, salt and pepper to a small glass. Stir to combine, then crack the egg and separate the yolk before dropping it into the mixture raw and downing the whole thing.

BLOODY DERBY

A Bloody Derby is a Snapper containing bourbon. I've got a bit of an ace up my sleeve with this one, though, and that's to infuse the bourbon with bacon before you use it in the snapper. Yes, *bacon*. The process to achieve this is called 'fat-washing', and yes, it sounds a bit disgusting, but the results are spectacular. Trust me on this one.

The technique of fat-washing was popularised by Don Lee at the world-famous Please Don't Tell (PDT) bar in New York in the mid-2000s. He learned the technique from, and was inspired by another bartender, Eben Freeman, who had used the technique to infuse rum with brown butter. However, it was Lee's cocktail, called the Benton Old-fashioned and served at PDT, that really put fat-washing as a technique into the minds of bartenders around the globe.

To make a fat-washed spirit, you need to take a fat that has flavour, place it into a vessel with your chosen spirit, leave it to infuse for a few hours, then freeze it to solidify the fat, making it easy to separate the two. Fat is a wonderful carrier of flavour, and consequently your spirit will be left infused with whatever flavour the fat had. You can use this technique to infuse spirits with oils and fats that already have flavour, like sesame oil or chicken fat, or use a plain oil to fry foods (e.g. bacon) in order to create a flavoured fat or oil.

To make bacon-fat-washed bourbon: Fry 10–20 rashers of streaky bacon in a little neutral oil or butter until the fat renders. Drain off the fat and set aside. Eat the bacon for breakfast (or set aside to use as a garnish for your cocktail). Use 1oz (25g) of bacon fat per 750ml bottle of bourbon and place in a sealed container. Leave to infuse for 4 hours, then place in the freezer for a couple of hours, or overnight. Strain the liquid to remove the solidified fat.

BLOODY JOSEPH

A Bloody Joseph is a snapper made with whisky. I recommend using a blended whisky for the majority of the drink, and then using a small amount of smoky or peated whisky as a float or accent within the main mix, to create a complex snapper with character. A whisky snapper can handle strong flavours more than most, especially when you're using a strongly-flavoured whisky as the 'accent'; therefore this is a great one to try with beef consommé or bouillon.

BLOODY FAIRY

A Bloody Fairy is a snapper made with absinthe. Be careful about how much absinthe you add or it will give a bitter edge to the drink. If this means that there's not much of an alcohol base to the drink, you can always add more vodka.

Coconut,
cream and egg

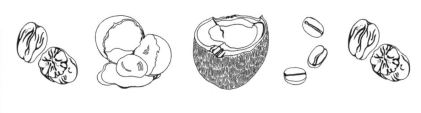

What a name for a chapter, hey? It may sound a little bizarre, but the cocktails in this column all have an inherent creaminess to them, both in terms of texture and taste, which come from the addition of either coconut cream, cream or a whole egg.

Tending to be quite rich, these aren't cocktails you can drink all night, but they also tend to get a bad press in today's obsession with healthy eating and drinking – and undeservedly so. I'm from the school of thought that a little bit of what you like never did anyone any harm, and these cocktails are beautifully balanced and wonderfully tasty.

The flips in particular are a category of cocktail that I wish were better known. Consisting of a spirit, sugar, spice and whole egg, it's the egg that tends to put people off. But trust me: don't knock one until you've tried one!

Column 10

66 7 **Bm** Bloody Mary	**73** 3 **Wr** White Russian
67 7 **Rs** Red Snapper	**74** 3 **Ax** Alexander
68 7 **Cu** Cubanita	**75** 3 **Pc** Piña Colada
69 11 **Ba** Bandera	**76** 5 **Df** Death Flip
70 7 **Po** Prairie Oyster	**77** 6 **Eg** Eggnog
	78 3 **Ru** Rum Flip
71 8 **Bd** Bloody Derby	**79** 4 **Bo** Boston Flip
72 7 **Bj** Bloody Joseph	**80** 4 **Ic** Irish Coffee

73 | 3
Wr
White
Russian

WHITE RUSSIAN

Sister to the Black Russian, both black and white Russians originate in America, named 'Russians' due to the use of vodka in both. Which came first? The jury's out on that one. But, as with most cocktails, the White Russian evolved through other drinks with bizarre names like the 'Barbara' and 'Russian Bear', before finally emerging as the cocktail we know and love today.

The first mentions of the White Russian in print were for advertisements for a coffee liqueur called Coffee Southern, a brand that, sadly, no longer exists. These appeared in newspapers in the States in 1965, alongside recipes for other cocktails, including a Southern Grasshopper.

For such a simple cocktail of just three parts, many dispute how best to make it. Do you take the vodka, coffee liqueur and cream and shake them all together? Or do you just shake the vodka and liqueur before floating the cream on top? Should the cream then be whipped? Should you shake at all? There are pros and cons to all. Firstly, shaking the cream is going to thicken it to some extent; however, if you're shaking over ice it will also dilute it – a bit of a balancing act for sure. If you layer the cream, it has the benefit of giving a silky-smooth mouthfeel over the alcohol that sits below it.

Personally, I think that the beauty of the White Russian lies, like the Negroni (see page 66), in its simplicity, both in terms of the ingredients and the method used. I therefore add the vodka and coffee liqueur to a glass with ice, give it a quick stir, then add the cream on top. A must, though, is the nutmeg on top, preferably freshly grated. It gives the cocktail the most wonderful aroma and makes it irresistible.

Feel free to amend the proportions of each ingredient in the cocktail to suit your taste. As liqueurs are lighter than spirits on the ABV, I recommend using a greater proportion of the vodka in relation to the liqueur. In terms of the cream, if you're on a diet, then skip the White Russian altogether. Please don't mess around with low-calorie cream or substituting with milk – it's just not the same.

Oh, and to make a Black Russian, just leave out the cream. Never, never add Coca-Cola. That's just plain wrong.

Ingredients   40ml vodka
20ml coffee liqueur
20ml single or whipping cream

Method   Add the vodka and coffee liqueur to a rocks glass filled with ice. Stir briefly to mix. Slowly pour the cream on top. Garnish with freshly grated nutmeg.

ALEXANDER

The Alexander is a cocktail consisting of spirit, cocoa liqueur and cream, the most famous of which being the Brandy Alexander. The origins of the Alexander, however, lie in gin. A recipe in Hugo R. Ensslin's *Recipes for Mixed Drinks* (1916), the first mention of the drink in a cocktail publication, calls for equal measures of gin, crème de cacao and cream. The Alexander is also mentioned in print before this, in October 1915 in *The Philadelphia Inquirer*: 'The head bartender has even gone so far as to invent an Alexander cocktail, which he is reserving to be served during the World Series.'

Baseball's World Series was in full swing at the time, and the bartender, wherever he worked, had created the cocktail in honour of Philadelphia pitcher Grover Cleveland Alexander. Sadly, the Boston Red Sox went on to beat the Philadelphia Phillies four games to one in the 1915 series. However, at least we gained a tasty cocktail out of it!

The recipe on page 108 is for a gin Alexander, but the formula works beautifully with other spirits, including brandy (or Cognac), whisky and rum – just swap them directly in place of the gin. The classic ratios were 1:1:1; however, it works a little better for me (and my waistline) with a little more gin and a little less cream. There are also numerous types of crème de cacao on the market. I prefer to use a white, uncoloured cacao as it leaves the cocktail a clean shade of white, rather than incorporating yellow or brown hues into the mix. That said, if you've only got coloured cacao at home, I'd still use it as it's still going to taste the same: delicious. As with the White Russian, the grated nutmeg on the top is a must, and it really needs to be freshly grated; it transforms the drink into something quite special.

When Prohibition hit America in 1919, the Alexander became a favourite drink, because it helped to disguise the quality of the homemade spirits (especially gin) that were being produced.

Ingredients
40ml gin
25ml crème de cacao
20ml single cream

Method
Pour all the ingredients into a cocktail shaker. Add ice and shake well. Double-strain into a chilled Martini glass or Champagne coupe. Garnish with freshly grated nutmeg.

PIÑA COLADA

The Piña Colada is ever-so-slightly-naff, yet loved by many. It's the cocktail that was immortalised by Rupert Holmes in *Escape (The Piña Colada Song)* released in 1979, which is definitely one of my guilty pleasures, music-wise! It's also the national drink of Puerto Rico – at least it has been since 1978. And, when made well, it is a cracking cocktail.

Three Puerto Rican bartenders – Ramón 'Monchito' Marrero Pérez, Ricardo García and Ramón Portas Mingot – each claim they invented the Piña Colada around the same time that a brand of coconut cream, Coco López, was created on the island. Coconut is key to the Piña Colada, as is the pineapple juice, which should be freshly pressed if possible; the name Piña Colada translates as 'strained pineapple' after all.

There are two main ways to make a Piña Colada, and both have their advantages and disadvantages. Firstly, you can shake all of the ingredients together before straining into a glass filled with ice. The advantages of this? You've probably got a cocktail shaker or equivalent to hand. The other way is to use a blender, which you may not have at home (I don't; my kitchen is too small). However, a blended Piña Colada does benefit from the thorough mix, so if you have a blender do give it a go. When blended the ice is much better incorporated into the drink, and you can add fresh pineapple into the mix. I also sometimes use coconut-flavoured rum in place of the traditional white rum to give an extra coconut hit.

Ingredients
50ml white rum
50ml coconut cream
150ml pineapple juice

Method
Shaken: Add all the ingredients to a cocktail shaker. Add ice and shake well. Strain into a highball or hurricane glass filled with ice.
Blended: Add all the ingredients to a blender (with optional fresh pineapple chunks). Add crushed ice and blend until smooth. Pour into a highball or hurricane glass.
Garnish: You've got to have fun with a Piña Colada, so throw all of the classic tiki (see Glossary, page 143) garnishes at it, from paper umbrellas to pineapple leaves, cherries, plastic monkeys dangling off the side.

DEATH FLIP

Taken from *Difford's Guide for Discerning Drinkers* (www. diffordsguide.com), the Death Flip sounds bonkers on paper (yes, it does contain a shot of Jägermeister), but trust me: it works surprisingly well. The resulting cocktail has bitter and herbal edges, which are rounded out by the creaminess of the egg. It was created in 2010 by Chris Hystead at the Black Pearl, a world-renowned cocktail bar located in Melbourne, Australia.

Ingredients   25ml tequila
25ml Jägermeister
25ml yellow Chartreuse
5ml sugar syrup (see Glossary, page 143)
1 egg

Method   Add all the ingredients to a cocktail shaker (crack the egg directly in). Shake without ice (dry shake), then add ice and shake again (wet shake). Double-strain into a chilled Martini glass or Champagne coupe and garnish with freshly grated nutmeg.

EGGNOG

A cocktail that started life in Europe, eggnog was drunk as a toast to health, but predominantly by the upper classes only as eggs were scarce. It's likely that the drink came about as an evolution of posset, a hot milky drink popular in the early medieval era.

Its association with Christmas came about when the drink made its way to America in the 1700s. Consequently, you can now buy the stuff ready-made in cartons during the run-up to Christmas; however, I'd *strongly* recommend making your own: the ready-made versions tend to be overly sweet.

It's not the simplest of drinks to make, so why not make it as a large punch for many people, as the effort per drink will be vastly reduced. As for the alcohol you put in it, anything goes, really. Purists will say that it must be bourbon, whiskey, or whiskey and rum, but I quite like it with Sherry or Madeira (this has the added advantage of reducing the overall ABV).

Ingredients   (serves 20)
200g sugar
24 eggs
750ml Cognac
250ml dark rum
1 litre double cream
1 litre full-fat milk

Method   Take a large mixing bowl or punchbowl. Whisk the sugar into the eggs and beat in the alcohol. Add the cream and beat again. Add the milk and beat a final time. Ladle into ice-filled glasses. Garnish each glass with freshly grated nutmeg just before serving.

RUM FLIP AND BOSTON FLIP

A flip is a family of drinks, first conceived in the late 1600s, when it consisted of beer, rum and sugar, heated with a hot iron from the fire. Flips first appeared in a cocktail book in *Jerry Thomas' Bartenders Guide or How to Mix Drinks: The Bon Vivant's Companion* (1862), where he listed recipes for 17 different flips, with varying different 'base' ingredients, from rum to brandy, gin, whisky, Port, Sherry, and ale. Thomas states that:

The essential in flips of all sorts is to produce the smoothness by repeated pouring back and forward between two vessels and beating up the eggs well in the first instance, the sweetening and spices according to taste.

The basic formula for a 'modern' flip is spirit or fortified wine, whole egg and sugar. They can sometimes contain cream (although traditionally they didn't).

Rum Flip   50ml rum
25ml sugar syrup (see Glossary, page 143)
1 egg

Boston Flip   50ml bourbon
50ml Madeira
10ml sugar syrup (see Glossary, page 143)
1 egg

Method   Add all the ingredients to a cocktail shaker (crack the egg directly in). Shake without ice (dry shake), then add ice and shake again (wet shake). Double-strain into a chilled Martini glass or Champagne coupe and garnish with freshly grated nutmeg.

80   4

Ic
Irish Coffee

IRISH COFFEE

The story of the Irish Coffee begins in Foynes Airbase
(now Shannon Airport), on Ireland's western coast.
A bartender there named Joe Sheridan made one
for Stanton Delaplane, a writer for the *San Francisco
Chronicle*. Delaplane was so impressed by the drink
that he introduced it to his local bar back home: the
Buena Vista Café. The owners and bartenders shared
Delaplane's enthusiasm and spent hours of research,
trying to perfect the recipe.

The glass used to serve your Irish Coffee is
important, due to the fact that the liquid is going to be
hot. You could serve it in a mug, but that means you
couldn't see the cocktail's cream float, which would be
a shame. In terms of glasses, a toddy glass is preferred
(it's a handled, heatproof glass), but you can use a
stemmed wine glass so long as it's heatproof; you'll then
be able to hold the glass by the stem, so you shouldn't
burn your fingers.

As for the whiskey, the Dead Rabbit in New York,
a world-famous cocktail bar that's known for its Irish
Coffees (still the best I've tasted to date), uses a blend
like Jameson's in its downstairs bar, but opts for a heavier
pot-still Irish whiskey when making them upstairs in the
cocktail-driven Parlour bar. It's interesting to see how
the choice of whiskey affects the flavour of this cocktail,
even with the strong flavour of the coffee.

The Dead Rabbit, through countless experiments,
insists that the key to a truly great Irish Coffee is to keep
the coffee at 78°C; they use a fancy immersion circulator
favoured by chefs to achieve this. I'm not advocating
for anyone to go out and buy this type of kit, but bear in
mind that the coffee shouldn't be piping hot; it helps the
cream to layer better at this slightly cooler temperature.

To float the cream, it's easier if you slightly whip it by
shaking it (without ice) first. Then, hold a spoon at the
top of the coffee, against the glass, and pour the cream
slowly into the bowl of the spoon. What's crucial with an

Irish Coffee is that you never, EVER, use squirty cream from a can.

The Dead Rabbit has taken inspiration from other cocktails of this style (such as the Alexander, Eggnog and Flip, within this chapter) and garnishes its Irish Coffees with a fresh grating of nutmeg. Having tried it, I'm a huge advocate, and subsequently now feel that something is lacking if I don't include it.

Ingredients

whipping cream
50ml Irish whiskey
25ml muscovado sugar syrup (see Glossary, page 143)
filtered coffee

Method

Add hot water to your glass to warm it. Lightly whip the cream by shaking it in a cocktail shaker (no ice). Empty the water from the glass and pour in the whiskey and sugar syrup, then fill with coffee until the glass is around three-quarters full. Stir briefly to mix. Using the technique described opposite, float the cream on top of the coffee.

Absinthe

The first row of the 'rare earth' elements separated at the bottom of the table contains absinthe cocktails. Because absinthe is such a distinctively flavoured spirit (and strong to boot), not all of the cocktails in this row are absinthe-dominant. However, what they all showcase is the flavour and versatility of absinthe as a cocktail ingredient.

Absinthe was a popular ingredient in classic cocktails, allowing interesting herbal flavours to be incorporated into drinks. Seminal cocktail books like *The Savoy Cocktail Book* by Harry Craddock (1930) contain huge numbers of cocktails featuring the 'green fairy' (absinthe's nickname); in fact the Savoy's book lists over 100. The cocktails in this chapter are a mix of these classics, plus one or two more recent discoveries.

SAZERAC

81	5
Sz	
Sazerac	

Another New Orleans classic, the Sazerac cocktail wasn't put into print until the early 20th century, yet it's certain that the drink is much older than that. A mix of Cognac, rye whiskey, sugar and absinthe, it's a potent cocktail which, when made properly, is like liquid gold in a glass – provided you like strong flavours. It's a unique cocktail in that it's traditionally served in a rocks glass, but without the rocks (ice). A Sazerac served on ice should therefore be sent back.

In the 1948 cocktail book *The Fine Art of Mixing Drinks*, author David A. Embury describes the Sazerac as 'merely an Old-fashioned made with Peychaud's bitters instead of Angostura and flavoured with a dash of Absinthe'. While he is technically correct, the substitution of Angostura for Peychaud's bitters, and the addition of absinthe, transform the drink into something much more complex than the Old-fashioned. The herbal notes from the absinthe in particular really work against the strong booze (whether you're using rye, Cognac or a mix of the two) to freshen and lift, as does the lemon-peel twist – just be sure to discard it, or else it will float around looking quite lost in your glass due to the lack of ice: not a good look.

A Sazerac can be made with either rye whiskey, Cognac, or a blend of the two. I personally like mine 50:50, as I think the balance between the sweetness of the Cognac and the spiciness of the rye is perfect at this ratio. But so long as there's a good measure (50ml) of spirit, the ratios are yours to play around with.

Ingredients
25ml rye whiskey
25ml Cognac
10ml sugar syrup (see Glossary, page 143)
3 dashes Peychaud's bitters
2 dashes absinthe

Method
Fill a rocks glass with crushed ice to chill it. Add the rye, Cognac, sugar syrup and Peychaud's bitters to a mixing glass with ice and stir gently to dilute. Empty the rocks glass, then add a couple of dashes of absinthe. Swirl the absinthe around the chilled glass to coat it and discard any excess. Check the dilution of the cocktail in the mixing glass and stir further if required. Strain into the absinthe-washed glass. Garnish with a twist of lemon, but be sure to discard it.

82   4
Rm
Remember
the Maine

REMEMBER THE MAINE

The Remember the Maine sits somewhere between a Manhattan and a Sazerac. It first appeared in *The Gentleman's Companion* (1939), written by Charles H. Baker. Named after the 1898 sinking of the *USS Maine*, an American battleship, which started the Spanish-American War, this is a cocktail to be taken seriously.

Unlike the Sazerac, the Remember the Maine is served in a Martini glass or Champagne coupe, with a lemon twist. Baker includes very clear and amusing instructions to make it: 'Stir briskly in clockwise fashion – this makes it sea going, presumably!'

Ingredients   50ml rye whiskey
20ml sweet vermouth
10ml cherry brandy
2 dashes absinthe

Method   Add all the ingredients to a mixing glass and fill with ice. Stir until properly diluted (clockwise, if you like) and strain into a chilled Martini glass or Champagne coupe. Garnish with a lemon twist.

83   5
Cr
Corpse
Reviver #2

CORPSE REVIVER #2

The Corpse Reviver family of cocktails is intended to be morning-enlivener cocktails as the name suggests – so much so they're capable of reviving the dead. Perhaps not, but a great name nonetheless. First listed in the 1871 cocktail publication *The Gentleman's Table Guide* by E. Ricket and C. Thomas, the reviver family has been around for a while. It wasn't until *The Savoy Cocktail Book* (by Harry Craddock) in 1930, however, that the #2 version appeared.

While a family of cocktails by name, there isn't that much to connect the cocktails to each other. The Corpse Reviver (or #1) is a mix of Cognac, Calvados and sweet vermouth, whereas the #2 consists of gin, lemon juice, triple sec, Lillet and absinthe. My preference very much sits with the #2 – as do most people's, if modern bar menus are anything to go by. It's very rare that you'll see a Corpse Reviver listed with anything other than a #2 at the end!

The recipe originally calls for the now-discontinued Kina Lillet vermouth (as with the Vesper; see page 10). It's therefore recommended to use Lillet Blanc as the nearest substitute.

Refreshing, tart and very sippable, the Corpse Reviver #2 is one of my favourite gin cocktails. Dangerously drinkable, given the amount of alcohol it contains, perhaps now is a good time to share Craddock's wise (and amusing) words: 'Four taken in swift succession will quickly unrevive the corpse again.' Quite.

Ingredients   25ml gin
25ml triple sec
25ml Lillet Blanc vermouth
25ml lemon juice
2–3 dashes absinthe

Method   Add all the ingredients to a cocktail shaker. Add ice and
shake well. Double-strain into a Martini glass or
Champagne coupe. Garnish with a twist of lemon zest.

84   5
Gf
Green Fairy

GREEN FAIRY

The Green Fairy cocktail takes its name from the common
nickname for absinthe, *La Fée Verte*, or green fairy. It is
referred to as such in countless books, poems and songs
throughout history, as absinthe was celebrated as many
an artist's muse.

The Green Fairy cocktail is basically an absinthe sour.
It was created in the 1990s by Dick Bradsell in London (yes,
another brilliant classic cocktail invented by Bradsell).

Over the past few years, there have been many new
brands of absinthe appearing on the market. Some of
this has to do with the fact that the US ban on absinthe
was overturned in 2007, opening up a new market, but
it's also partly due to an increased interest in classic
cocktails, many of which contained the green spirit. For
this reason, you'll also find some new products that are
actually reverse-engineered from classic absinthe bottles
producers have found, striving to recreate the flavour
of the absinthes of the past, and therefore the classic
cocktails made with them.

Given the strength of most absinthes, the cocktail
recipe included on page 120 (taken from *Difford's Guide
for Discerning Drinkers*, www.diffordsguide.com) only
features a single shot of the spirit; it also includes chilled
water to reduce the ABV and ensure that the flavour of
absinthe comes through: it's a spirit that comes to life
with a little dilution.

While the original created by Bradsell was served
straight up, you can also serve this on the rocks.

Ingredients	25ml absinthe
	25ml chilled water
	25ml lemon juice
	20ml sugar syrup (see Glossary, page 143)
	1 dash Angostura bitters
	½ egg white
Method	Add all the ingredients to a cocktail shaker. Shake without ice (dry shake), then add ice and shake again (wet shake). Strain into a chilled Martini glass or Champagne coupe. Garnish with a twist of lemon zest.

MONKEY GLAND

Created in the 1920s, the Monkey Gland is a classic cocktail that balances gin and fresh (note the word 'fresh': this is important!) orange juice with absinthe and grenadine. Credited to Harry MacElhone, the famed proprietor of Harry's New York Bar in Paris, he named the cocktail after experiments conducted on monkeys by surgeon Serge Voronoff. The experiments were specifically to do with transplanting testicles from male monkeys into male humans to improve their sex drive. What a thing to name a drink after! Still, it grabbed people's attention, and was covered in many newspapers, including *The Washington Post* in 1923.

Ingredients	50ml gin
	30ml orange juice
	5ml grenadine
	1–2 dashes absinthe
Method	Add all the ingredients to a cocktail shaker. Add ice and shake well. Double-strain into a chilled Martini glass or Champagne coupe. Garnish with a twist of orange zest.

CONCEALED WEAPON

The Concealed Weapon adds another dimension – fruit – to the sour formula. The fruit, in the form of black raspberry liqueur, Chambord, marries surprisingly well with the absinthe, and the sour staples of lemon and egg white tie it all together in a tasty, yet potent (due to the ABV of absinthe) cocktail. Created in 2000 by London bartender Danny Smith, this recipe is taken from *Difford's Guide for Discerning Drinkers,* www.diffordsguide.com. Given the similarities to the Green Fairy (see page 119), and the timings of both cocktails' creations, it's more than likely that it was inspired by Bradsell's Absinthe Sour.

Ingredients

25ml absinthe
25ml Chambord liqueur
20ml lemon juice
15ml sugar syrup (see Glossary, page 143)
1 dash Angostura bitters
1 dash Peychaud's bitters
½ egg white

Method

Add all the ingredients to a cocktail shaker. Shake without ice (dry shake), then add ice and shake again (wet shake). Strain into a chilled Martini glass or Champagne coupe. Garnish with a twist of lemon zest.

87 3
Af
Absinth
Frappé

ABSINTHE FRAPPÉ

When absinthe made its way from France and Europe over to the States, few places embraced it as strongly as New Orleans. In 1874, The Absinthe Room was famous for serving the spirit in the French-style, using absinthe fountains to dilute it. That's right: no setting it on fire, and no shooting it straight. Bartender and owner Cayetano Ferrer developed the Absinthe Frappé as a refreshing way to drink the spirit. Given the summer heat and humidity in NOLA, as New Orleans is known, it's not surprising that it caught on.

Anisette is an anise-flavoured liqueur made by distilling aniseed. It is colourless and sweeter than most other aniseed-based products. If you want to remain authentic to the French roots of this frappé (despite it being created in the States), then Marie Brizard Anisette is the brand to seek out.

Ingredients   50ml absinthe
20ml anisette
soda water

Method   Fill a rocks glass with crushed ice. Add the absinthe, anisette and a splash of soda water. Churn with a bar spoon to mix and add more crushed ice to fill the glass, if needed. Taste and top with more soda water to taste.

DEATH IN THE AFTERNOON

The Death in the Afternoon was created by renowned imbiber Ernest Hemingway, its name taken from his 1932 book of the same name. To make it, Hemingway said you should:

Pour one jigger absinthe into a Champagne glass. Add iced Champagne until it attains the proper opalescent milkiness. Drink three to five of these slowly.

Three to five?! Told you he was a renowned imbiber! I prefer more modern versions of the cocktail, which feature a little less absinthe, alongside lemon juice and sugar syrup. The citrus not only helps to take the edge off the absinthe, but also creates a more refreshing cocktail.

Ingredients   15ml absinthe
20ml lemon juice
10ml sugar syrup (see Glossary, page 143)
Champagne

Method   Add the absinthe, lemon juice and sugar syrup to a cocktail shaker. Add ice and shake well. Strain into a chilled Champagne glass and top up with Champagne.

BLOODY FAIRY

See page 102 and from pages 93–102 for more on snappers.

90 6
As
**Absinthe
Suissesse**

ABSINTHE SUISSESSE

A great brunch cocktail, not only for its refreshing flavour and texture, but also for its hangover-banishing properties. This is yet another absinthe cocktail to come out of New Orleans. In terms of the crème de menthe, you have two options: green or colourless. It depends how much of a green tinge you would like in your final cocktail as to which you use; there will be no effect on flavour.

Ingredients
40ml absinthe
10ml crème de menthe
5ml orgeat syrup
1 egg white
15ml single cream
15ml full-fat milk

Method
Add all the ingredients to a cocktail shaker. Shake without ice (dry shake), then add ice and shake again (wet shake). Strain into a highball glass over ice.

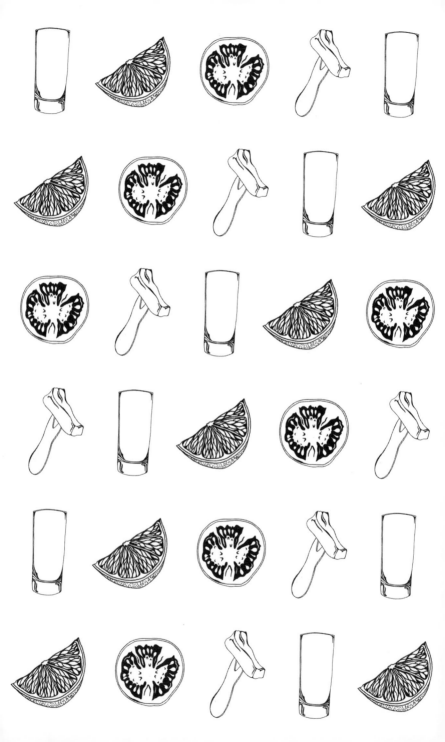

Beer

Beer cocktails: now there's something you don't hear every day. They've rather fallen out of favour in recent times, reminiscent of house parties where you add anything you have to a punchbowl and some idiot throws in a can of lager – usually Stella. However, beer cocktails have a long and prestigious history within the cocktail world. Ales and porters were used in drinks like the classic Purl to lengthen a cocktail while providing depth and a complexity of flavour. The drinks in this row of the table are therefore both a tribute to, and examples of, this vein and so are well worth a try. They also contain a few tasty citrus-based cocktails with lagers, because Mexican lager and citrus go together like gin and tonic. Trust me.

91   5

Sj

St James's
Gate

ST JAMES'S GATE

Named after the location of the Guinness headquarters in Dublin, the St James's Gate is a cocktail created by Tony Conigliaro at his bar, 69 Colebrooke Row, in London. Cocktails at 69 Colebrooke Row, also known as 'The Bar With No Name', start life in a laboratory, where they explore and dissect flavours using scientific methods and techniques. The St James's Gate is unique, then, in that it is possible to make it at home with relative ease.

A twist on a rum sour, the St James's Gate is a velvety mix of dark rum (Myers rum is recommended), and uses a Guinness reduction alongside the usual lemon, sugar and egg white sour formula.

Ingredients   50ml dark rum (Myers recommended)
25ml lemon juice
20ml Guinness reduction (see opposite)
15ml sugar syrup (see Glossary, page 143)
egg white

Method   Add all the ingredients to a cocktail shaker. Shake without ice (dry shake), then add ice and shake again (wet shake). Strain into a chilled Martini glass or Champagne coupe.

For the Guinness reduction

Pour a can of Guinness into a saucepan with a couple of teaspoons of black treacle. Simmer over a low heat until reduced to a syrup.

LAGERITA

The Lagerita is just one of many beer cocktails based on classic cocktails with a citrus backbone, including the Maquiri (a Daiquiri with lager), B'loma (a Paloma topped with beer) and the Sagres Hemingway (a Hemingway Daiquiri topped with lager).

The Lagerita, a Margarita topped with Mexican beer, turns what is already a refreshing cocktail into a longer summertime drink. Mexican beer and citrus are great bedfellows – just ask anyone who puts lime in a Corona! Adding tequila imparts strength and power to the drink. Whether to salt the rim of the glass or not is up to you.

Ingredients
50ml tequila
30ml lime juice
25ml triple sec or curaçao
Mexican beer

Method
Add the tequila, lime juice and triple sec to a cocktail shaker. Add ice and shake well. Strain into a highball glass or half-pint glass filled with ice (salt rim optional). Top with beer. Garnish with a lime zest, slice or wheel.

DE BEAUVOIR

The De Beauvoir cocktail is evidence of the recent resurgence of beer cocktails. In 2013, during London Cocktail Week, www.diffordsguide.com hosted a dedicated Beer-tail cocktail competition.

The De Beauvoir was created especially for this competition by London bartender Andrea Montague. A fan of the Beavertown Brewery's range of beers, and especially its smoked porter called Smog Rocket, she used that as the starting point. She then paired it with bourbon, a hazelnut liqueur, lemon juice and whisky-barrel-aged bitters produced by Fee Brothers. If you can't get hold of any of the whisky-barrel-aged bitters (they are quite specific), then it's best to leave them out.

Named after the area of London, De Beauvoir Town, near to where the Beavertown Brewery is located, the cocktail went on to win the competition. You'll understand why when you try it.

Ingredients

30ml bourbon
15ml Frangelico (hazelnut liqueur)
15ml lemon juice
30ml smoked porter
5ml sugar syrup (see Glossary, page 143)
1 dash Fee Brothers Whiskey Barrel-Aged Bitters

Method

Add all the ingredients to a cocktail shaker. Add ice and shake well. Strain into a chilled Champagne coupe.

94   4
Sp
Shaky Pete's
Ginger Brew

SHAKY PETE'S GINGER BREW

A cocktail created by Pete Jeary (aka Shaky Pete) during his time working at Hawksmoor, Seven Dials, in London. A blend of gin, lemon juice, ginger syrup and beer, it's a long and refreshing cocktail that pairs perfectly with a Hawksmoor burger, and makes a hell of a brunch-time drink to blow away the cobwebs. If you've ever tried a shandy made with ginger beer, you'll recognise the concept; however, the strength of the gin and the freshness of the lemon juice raise this cocktail to a new level. The cocktail was created with London Pride beer, but any well-rounded ale will work.

It's worth taking the time to make your own ginger syrup if you can (recipe opposite), as it retains much more of the spicy and fiery elements from the ginger than commercially-produced versions.

Ingredients

40ml gin
50ml lemon juice
50ml ginger syrup (see opposite)
beer (ale)

Method   Add the gin, lemon juice and ginger syrup to a blender with a couple of ice cubes. Blend. Fine-strain the mixture into a chilled pint glass. Top up with beer.

For the ginger syrup

Take 250g peeled and chopped fresh root ginger, 250g caster sugar and 125ml water. Blend together and fine-strain into a bottle to store until needed.

BEST BOWER

As with Andrea Montague's De Beauvoir, the Best Bower combines whisky with beer – this time, however, rye whiskey is the star of the show. A cocktail created by London bartender Bobby Hiddleston, it's topped with the lighter Saison beer and also features tea. The 5ml of Suze adds a bitter edge that works beautifully with the tea and lemon juice.

Ingredients   40ml rye whiskey
15ml lemon juice
20ml rooibos tea syrup (see below)
5ml Suze liqueur
Saison pale ale

Method   Combine the rye, lemon juice, tea syrup and Suze in a cocktail shaker. Add ice and shake well. Strain into a highball glass filled with ice and top up with Saison.

For the tea syrup

Add 2 rooibos tea bags to 250ml hot water. Leave to infuse for 3–4 minutes. Take out the teabags and stir in an equal volume of sugar to create a 1:1 syrup.

DRINK WITH NO NAME

London-based bartender Oskar Kinberg is a huge advocate of beer cocktails. At his bar underneath the Michelin-starred Dabbous restaurant in Soho, he has dedicated a whole section of his menu to them.

A native of Sweden, he grew up drinking a drink called *mumma* at Christmas-time. *Mumma* is normally a mix of gin, porter, lager, Madeira and spices, but each family has its own recipe, and there's a vast difference between them.

Oskar's Drink with No Name cocktail combines bourbon, lemon juice, agave syrup, ginger ale and greengage liqueur. Greengages are a type of plum that are sweet and rich in flavour. The greengage liqueur used in Oskar's recipe is made by Bramley & Gage. If you can't get hold of any, then substitute it with a couple of teaspoons of greengage jam – or plum jam at a push.

Ingredients
25ml bourbon
25ml greengage liqueur
15ml lemon juice
10ml agave syrup
50ml ginger ale
lager

Method
Add the bourbon, greengage liqueur, lemon juice and agave syrup to a cocktail shaker. Add ice and shake well. Strain into a highball or half-pint glass filled with ice. Top with the ginger ale and lager.

97 7
Ac
Ale of Two Cities

ALE OF TWO CITIES

The Ale of Two Cities was the winning drink of a worldwide cocktail competition hosted by 42Below vodka. Held in his home country of New Zealand, the cocktail was created by Sean Ware for Team GB for the 2008 competition. OK, so there technically isn't any beer in this one, but it's a damn tasty drink and it's served in an old-school British half-pint glass: close enough? Please forgive me...

The inspiration behind the drink was the good old English pub, classic literature, and the British love for all things boozy. The flavour combination was a little more unusual and punchy to see in cocktails but not uncommon in old punches or ales from the Victorian era.

The tankard half-pint glass is hugely reminiscent of a traditional British pub, and so fitted in with the cocktail concept perfectly. It's also the reason why the cocktail below has quite a large measure of booze in it in total: to ensure the glass isn't left half empty when you serve it!

Ingredients 20ml lime juice
15ml homemade nettle cordial (see below)
75ml cloudy apple juice
15ml malted barley syrup
75ml 42Below Feijoa Vodka
25ml Punt e Mes sweet vermouth
2 dashes Angostura bitters

Method Chill the tankard. Add the lime juice, nettle cordial, apple juice and malted barley syrup to a cocktail shaker or mixing glass. Stir to dissolve the thick malt syrup, then add the alcoholic ingredients, add plenty of ice and shake hard. Strain into the chilled tankard. Garnish with chips coated in salt, malted vinegar and a wooden chip fork. Standard!

For the nettle cordial

100g fresh nettle leaves
250g granulated sugar
10g citric acid
200ml water

Method Wash the nettles, removing any damaged leaves or thick stems, and roughly chop them. Add the sugar, citric acid and water to a saucepan and heat until boiling. Leave to cool to around 70°C. Add the chopped nettles and stir. Once cool, add the mixture to an airtight jar. Leave in a cool, dark place for 1–2 days, agitating or shaking it now and again. Strain through a sieve or piece of muslin if you have it. Add a shot (25ml) or so of vodka to help to preserve the cordial (but only if you're using it for boozy cocktails!) and it will last for 3–4 weeks in the fridge.

BLACK VELVET

The Black Velvet cocktail was created when Britain was in mourning after the death of HRH Prince Albert, husband of Queen Victoria. Devastated by his death, the Queen wore black for the rest of her life. Appropriate then, that the Champagne in the cocktail is shrouded by the Guinness, which turns the cocktail black.

Created in 1861 by a bartender at the Brooks's Club in London, it is made from stout (Guinness being the most easy-to-get-hold-of brand) and Champagne. What sounds like a bizarre combination is actually lovely. The Champagne cuts through the heaviness of the stout and the stout works well against the tartness of the Champagne.

Some recipes prescribe floating the stout on top of the Champagne, which is not only extra effort, but completely unnecessary. Why not make two with the time you'll save?

Ingredients Champagne
75ml Guinness

Method Pour the Champagne, then the stout carefully into a chilled Champagne glass. Stir briefly to mix.

MICHELADA

The Michelada is effectively a beer-based Bloody Mary. Consisting of beer, lime juice, spices and tomato juice, the cocktail is often served in a glass rimmed with salt. While their backbone remains the same, there are many different variations of the Michelada, featuring many different types of sauces and spices. These variations tend to depend on where the recipe comes from, and it can also be amended and customised to your individual tastes.

The recipe opposite is for a 'standard' Michelada, if such a thing exists. I like to add a twist to the salt rim of the cocktail by incorporating celery salt, or salt mixed

with dried chilli flakes. If you like, add an extra-boozy kick
by including tequila.

Ingredients   lime wedge
50ml tomato juice
hot pepper sauce
Worcestershire sauce
Mexican light beer

Method   Take the lime wedge and rub it around the rim of a
highball glass. Put a tablespoon or so of salt on to a
plate, then, holding the glass at a 90 degree angle to
the plate, coat the rim of the glass with the salt (the lime
juice will help it stick). Fill the glass with ice. Add the
tomato juice, a couple of dashes of hot pepper sauce
and Worcestershire sauce to taste. Top with beer, and
stir gently.

GUINNESS PUNCH

The Guinness Punch comes straight out of the Caribbean
– did you know they're huge fans of Guinness? Slightly
different versions of the cocktail exist as you move from
island to island, but the basic formula remains the same.
The key is to balance the bitter Guinness against the
sweetness of the condensed milk. Some don't add the
rum, but the extra punch adds depth to the cocktail and
stops it from being too sickly.

Ingredients   50ml rum
50ml condensed milk
200ml Guinness

Method   Blend all the ingredients with a scoop of crushed ice
until smooth. Serve in a rocks glass. Garnish with freshly
grated nutmeg.

Overproof

To end with the 'serious' stuff, the final chapter and row of the table features overproof spirits. Not just a way to get trollied quickly, the use of overproof spirit can add to, and enhance, a cocktail in a way that spirits with a 'standard' ABV just can't. Alcohol is a very good carrier of flavours; that's why most traditional alcohols like gin and absinthe exist: they were a way of extracting the 'goodness' from herbs and spices and preserving them in medicinal tinctures (they just had the added advantage of being downright delicious too). The higher the ABV of a spirit, the more flavour will come through. This can be an advantage and a disadvantage. In the case of these cocktails it's definitely an advantage, as it helps to give an extra dimension to the spirit – and not just because of the boozy kick!

NAVY MARTINI

A Navy Martini is simply a Martini made with a navy-strength gin. For full instructions on martinis, see page 6.

Navy-strength gin must be at least 57% ABV, and therefore overproof. The concept of navy-strength gins came about in the early 1800s, when the Royal British Navy carried gin on its ships. The gin and the rum on board was kept at 57% ABV, as at this strength it would enable gunpowder to light if doused in the spirit, which allowed its strength to be tested easily at sea, to make sure it hadn't been diluted.

To craft a Martini with a navy-strength gin, you need to be careful to chill and dilute the spirit properly, in order to mellow out the high ABV of the gin. For this reason, I also tend to drink these either wet or dirty, and make sure to choose a citrus-led gin like Plymouth.

Ingredients　　60ml navy-strength gin
20ml dry vermouth

Method　　Add the ingredients to a mixing glass filled with ice. Stir until well chilled and diluted. Strain into a chilled Martini glass or Champagne coupe. Garnish with a citrus zest twist (the type of citrus will depend on the brand of gin used).

NUCLEAR DAIQUIRI

The Nuclear Daiquiri was created by Gregor de Gruyther at LAB bar in London in 2005. It takes the Daiquiri formula of rum, lime and sugar and supercharges it. It also adds Chartreuse, which brings herbal elements to the cocktail, adding extra complexity. Despite the fact that it contains a full shot of overproof rum, it's a surprisingly drinkable cocktail.

When Gregor created the cocktail, he used Wray & Nephew white overproof rum, which is a distinctively flavoured overproof, so seek it out if possible. He also left it ungarnished, because 'No garnish can withstand the awesome power of the Nuclear Daiquiri.' It's certainly one hell of a cocktail.

Ingredients 25ml overproof white rum
25ml Green Chartreuse
25ml lime juice
10ml Velvet Falernum liqueur

Method Add all the ingredients to a cocktail shaker. Add ice and shake well to ensure the cocktail is adequately diluted and chilled. Double-strain into a cocktail glass or Champagne coupe.

GIMLET

The Gimlet is one of the original cocktails to use overproof spirit. How and when the cocktail was created is under dispute (perhaps those who came up with the drink had one too many?). What is known, however, is how the British officers in the navy adopted it as their own for its health benefit to sailors, as the vitamin C was a great way to ward off scurvy.

It's difficult to talk about the Gimlet without mentioning Rose's lime juice cordial specifically. Turning the lime juice into a cordial provided a way of keeping the lime juice consumable for long periods of time – crucial for long voyages at sea. The brand used was specifically Rose's, and while other lime juice cordials will do the trick, they're never quite the same.

Ingredients   50ml navy-strength gin
50ml Rose's lime juice cordial

Method   Add both ingredients to a mixing glass and stir. Strain into a chilled Martini glass or Champagne coupe.

TRINIDAD SOUR

The Trinidad Sour is a cocktail created in 2009 by New York bartender Giuseppe Gonzalez. It is a most unusual concept, as the drink contains a full shot of Angostura bitters (44.7% ABV), more commonly used in dashes and drops, the cocktail equivalent of salt and pepper.

So, what happens when you take something like Angostura and completely turn its use on its head by adding such a hefty measure? Well, the bitter notes and clove flavour come through most for me, but you get a wonderfully rich flavour, and bags of depth.

There are so many reasons why this cocktail shouldn't work, but it really does. To stand up to the bitters, the cocktail also includes the sweet orgeat syrup against lemon juice and a dash of rye whiskey. The resulting cocktail is complex, with layers of flavour provided both from the bitters and from the combination with the rye.

Ingredients   25ml Angostura bitters
25ml orgeat syrup
20ml lemon juice
15ml rye whiskey

Method   Put all the ingredients into a cocktail shaker. Add ice and shake well. Double-strain into a chilled Martini glass or Champagne coupe.

105	10
Z	
Zombie	

ZOMBIE

The Zombie, created by Don the Beachcomber, first appeared in 1934 as a hangover cure. The cocktail became especially popular at the Hurricane Bar at the 1939 New York World's Fair. The rule of no more than two per person was in place from the moment of its conception, due to the sheer volume of booze in the drink, not to mention the overproof rum float on top, and this still remains in place in many venues to this day.

Ingredients
20ml lemon juice
20ml lime juice
1 teaspoon sugar
20ml white rum
20ml golden rum
20ml dark rum
20ml pineapple juice
20ml passion fruit syrup
1 dash Angostura bitters
20ml overproof rum

Method
Add the lemon and lime juices to a cocktail shaker along with the sugar. Stir until dissolved. Add the rest of the ingredients except for the overproof rum, then fill with ice. Shake well and strain into a hurricane glass filled with cubed ice. Top with overproof rum and serve with a small pineapple wedge.

106	5
Nh	
Nuclear Hurricane	

NUCLEAR HURRICANE

The Nuclear Hurricane is a cross between a Nuclear Daiquiri (see page 137) and a Hurricane (see page 57). It's also flippin' delicious, and way too drinkable, given how much overproof rum there is in it. My first was in London bar NOLA, a New Orleans-styled bar located in Shoreditch. I've never looked back.

Ingredients
20ml overproof rum
20ml Green Chartreuse

20ml Velvet Falernum liqueur
25ml lime juice
50ml grapefruit soda (see page 87)

Method   Add all of the ingredients, except for the grapefruit soda, to a hurricane glass. Add crushed ice and churn with a bar spoon. Add more ice and churn again. Top with the grapefruit soda and more ice to form a cap. Garnish with a blown-out (and ideally slightly charred) cocktail umbrella!

Bartender's kit

A number of pieces of equipment are mentioned throughout this book. All are standard bartending staples; however, if you don't have them, or don't want to invest in them, below is a table listing some other solutions, including equipment found commonly in the kitchen that you can use in their absence.

ITEM	ALTERNATIVE FOUND IN YOUR KITCHEN
Bar spoon for measuring	Teaspoon (generally the right size: 5ml).
Bar spoon for stirring	Knife or chopstick, to enable easy stirring; most spoons will be too short, or the spoon end too large to allow easy stirring.
Citrus press	A standard citrus juicer, or your hands. *Tip:* microwave your citrus fruit for a couple of seconds, then roll it on a flat surface with the palm of your hand before juicing. This will make it much easier to extract the juice, especially when juicing by hand.
Citrus zester	Vegetable peeler or sharp knife (watch your fingers...).
Jigger:	Measuring spoons; so long as you're able to be accurate in your measurements, you can use any kit used for measuring liquids in the kitchen. The range of measuring spoons or angled measuring cups from OXO are particularly useful to have to hand when making cocktails as they allow for accurate measuring of many liquid volumes.
Mixing glass	Boston tin, measuring jug, glass jug, large jar... even a vase will work. You want a large receptacle that can hold a reasonable amount of ice, and still allow you to stir.
Muddler	Rolling pin or the handle of a wooden spoon.

Glossary

ABV Alcohol by volume: the standard measure of how much alcohol (ethanol) is in a specified amount of an alcoholic beverage such as a spirit, wine or liqueur.

Bar spoon A long-handled spoon, with a twisted middle section that can be useful for pouring liquids down in order to layer them. Bar spoons often have a flat disc at one end that can also be helpful for pressing or crushing ingredients.

Bruise Generally used to describe how to treat leaves such as mint in a cocktail. Bruising involves lightly agitating the leaf, NOT crushing it. Crushing leaves leads to chlorophyll being released, which gives drinks an unpleasant bitter taste.

Champagne coupe/ coupette A shallow, saucer-type glass popular in the 1930s, and currently enjoying a resurgence. Legend has it that it was modelled on the breast of Marie Antoinette – although it is now known that it was designed in England in 1663.

Cocktail glass Otherwise known as a Martini glass, it is the now-iconic V-shaped glass most people associate with the Martini cocktail. They're being used less and less these days, substituted in favour of the Champagne saucer or Champagne coupe in many bars.

Double-strain Strain your cocktail through a fine sieve to catch any pips from berries, or shards of ice from shaking a cocktail, etc.

Highball glass A tall tumbler glass, usually containing 250–350ml liquid.

Jigger A measure used to precisely add the required volumes of ingredients into a cocktail. Usually metal, they come in many sizes: commonly 25ml, 30ml, 50ml and 60ml.

Muddle   Crushing ingredients to release their juice. Commonly used with citrus fruit in built drinks, or berries before shaking (to ensure they're fully mixed with the other ingredients).

Rocks glass   A short tumbler glass, also called an Old-fashioned glass after the cocktail traditionally served in it.

Sling glass   A very tall, slim glass used for serving the Singapore Sling in the 1920s.

Sugar syrup   Essentially this is just sugar and water. Most recipes will require a mix in the ratio of 1:1 by volume. However, you may see the use of 2:1, referring to the use of double the sugar to the water. You can make these easily at home.

A 1:1 mix is possible using a blender; just add equal volumes of water and sugar to a blender and blend until well mixed.

To make a 2:1 syrup you will generally need heat to ensure the sugar dissolves in the water. Heat the water gently in a pan, add half of the sugar. Stir briefly and leave until the mixture becomes clear. Add the remaining sugar and repeat. Be careful not to over-stir; the mixture will clarify on its own if left, without agitation.

Tiki drink   'Tiki' is a term used to describe Polynesian-style cocktails, restaurants and bars. The cocktails are famously elaborate, mostly rum-based, and served in unusual glassware or serving vessels – everything from hollowed-out coconuts and pineapples to plastic volcanoes and pirate ships! They're often subject to over-the-top garnishes too. A lot of fun, so dig out your Hawaiian shirts and leis for tiki parties!

Zest/twist garnishes   Take a fresh piece of zest from the desired citrus fruit, hold it peel-down over the top of the glass (2–3cm away from the surface of the drink) and squeeze to express the oils over the top of the drink. Drop the peel into the drink, or discard if you prefer.

Further reading

Many of the older classics are available online as reprints and facsimile editions as well as in Kindle editions.

Baker, Charles H. *The Gentleman's Companion*. Echo Point Books, USA. 1939.

Bergeron, Victor Jules (Trader Vic). *Bartender's Guide by Trader Vic*. Garden City: 1947.

Berry, Jeff. *Beachbum Berry's Intoxica*. SLG Publishing, San Jose, CA: 2003

Byron, O. H. *The Modern Bartender's Guide*. 1884.

Craddock, Harry. *The Savoy Cocktail Book*. London: 1930.

Embury, David A. *The Fine Art of Mixing Drinks*. Garden City, NY: Doubleday, 1948.

Ensslin, Hugo R. *Recipes for Mixed Drinks*. USA: 1916.

Haigh, Ted. *Vintage Spirits and Forgotten Cocktails*. Quarry Books, Beverly, MA: 2009.

Johnson, Harry. *Harry Johnson's Bartenders' Manual*. USA: 1882.

Kappeler, George. *Modern American Drinks*. 1895.

MacElhone, Harry. *Harry's ABC of Mixing Cocktails*. USA: 1919.

MacElhone, Harry. *Barflies And Cocktails*. Lecram Press, NY:1927.

Mariani, John F. *The Encyclopedia of American Food and Drink*. 1983. New edition by Bloomsbury, USA: 2014.

Regan, Gary. *The Joy of Mixology: The Consummate Guide to the Bartender's Craft*. Random House, New York, NY: 2004.

Ricket, E. and C. Thomas. *The Gentleman's Table Guide*. Frederick Warne & Co: 1871.

Stuart, Thomas. *Stuart's Fancy Drinks And How To Mix Them*. 1896.

Tarling, William J. *Café Royal Cocktail Book.* United Kingdom Bartenders Guild, London: 1937

Thomas, Jerry. *Jerry Thomas' Bartenders Guide or How To Mix Drinks: The Bon Vivant's Companion.* USA: 1862.

Vermeire, Robert. *Cocktails: How to Mix Them.* USA: 1922.

Wondrich, David. *Imbibe!* Penguin Random House, New York, NY: 2007

Woon, Basil. *When It's Cocktail Time in Cuba.* H. Liveright, New York: 1928

On the web   *Difford's Guide for Discerning Drinkers –* www.diffordsguide.com

Gin Monkey – www.ginmonkey.co.uk

Acknowledgements

I would like to thank the following people for their help, advice, invaluable expertise and support throughout this process: Rebekkah Dooley, Leanne Garvie, Wendy Heydecke, Peter Holland, Hannah Lanfear, Andrea Montague, Siobhan Payne and Shayan Sanyal. To the countless others who have listened and advised over a drink or two along the way: I couldn't have done it without you. Special thanks also to Jamie Ambrose for her enormously helpful copywriting skills and Laura Higginson and the team at Ebury, who approached me to write this book. It has been a privilege and a pleasure!

Index